Shinto

PLATE 1 (see overleaf). OMIWA JINJA, NARA. Front view of the worshipping hall showing the offering box at the foot of the steps. In the upper foreground is the sacred rope suspended between the entrance pillars.

Shinto
THE KAMI WAY

by
DR. SOKYO ONO
Professor, Kokugakuin University
Lecturer, Association of Shinto Shrines

in collaboration with
WILLIAM P. WOODARD

sketches by
SADAO SAKAMOTO
Priest, Yasukuni Shrine

TUTTLE Publishing
Tokyo | Rutland, Vermont | Singapore

THE TUTTLE STORY
"Books to Span the East and West"

Our core mission at Tuttle Publishing is to create books which bring people together one page at a time. Tuttle was founded in 1832 in the small New England town of Rutland, Vermont (USA). Our fundamental values remain as strong today as they were then—to publish best-in-class books informing the English-speaking world about the countries and peoples of Asia. The world has become a smaller place today and Asia's economic, cultural and political influence has expanded, yet the need for meaningful dialogue and information about this diverse region has never been greater. Since 1948, Tuttle has been a leader in publishing books on the cultures, arts, cuisines, languages and literatures of Asia. Our authors and photographers have won numerous awards and Tuttle has published thousands of books on subjects ranging from martial arts to paper crafts. We welcome you to explore the wealth of information available on Asia at **www.tuttlepublishing.com**.

Published by Tuttle Publishing, an imprint of Periplus Editions (HK) Ltd.

www.tuttlepublishing.com

© 1962 by Charles E. Tuttle Publishing Company, Limited
All rights reserved

LCC Card No. 61014033
ISBN 978-0-8048-3557-2
ISBN 978-4-8053-1106-6 (for sale in Japan only)

First edition, 1962

Distributed by
Japan
Tuttle Publishing, Yaekari Building, 3rd Floor, 5-4-12 Osaki, Shinagawa-ku, Tokyo 141-0032
Tel: (81) 3 5437 0171 | Fax: (81) 3 5437 0755
sales@tuttle.co.jp | www.tuttle.co.jp

North America, Latin America & Europe
Tuttle Publishing, 364 Innovation Drive, North Clarendon, VT 05759-9436 USA
Tel: 1 (802) 773 8930 | Fax: 1 (802) 773 6993
info@tuttlepublishing.com | www.tuttlepublishing.com

Asia Pacific
Berkeley Books Pte. Ltd., 3 Kallang Sector #04-01, Singapore 349278
Tel: (65) 6741-2178 | Fax: (65) 67414-2179
inquiries@periplus.com.sg | www.tuttlepublishing.com

24 23 22 21 20   16 15 14 13 12
Japan 24 23 22 21 20   13 12 11 10 9
Printed in Singapore   2002TP

CONTENTS

Foreword vii

Preface ix

1 THE KAMI WAY 1

     Introduction, Mythology, Kami, Scriptures,
     Types of Shinto, Organization

II SHRINES 23

     Shrines and Shrine Paraphernalia, Precincts,
     Architecture, Priests and Shrine Functionaries,
     Parishes and Parishioners

III WORSHIP AND FESTIVALS 50

     Worship, Four Elements of Worship, Worship
     in the Home, Shrine Worship, Festivals

IV POLITICAL AND SOCIAL CHARACTERISTICS... 72

     Government Policy, the Arts, Economic Life,
     Relation with other Religions, Everyday Customs

V SOME SPIRITUAL CHARACTERISTICS 92

     Transmission of the Faith, Shrines and Nature;
     World, Man, Salvation and Death,
     Universality of Shinto

Index 113

FOREWORD

This book was first published in 1960 as Bulletin No. 8 of the International Institute for the Study of Religions, Tokyo, under the title *The Kami Way: An Introduction to Shrine Shinto.* The author, Dr. Sokyo Ono, professor of Kokugakuin University and lecturer for the Association of Shinto Shrines, compiled the material as a modern presentation of the meaning of Shrine Shinto to one who has devoted his entire professional life to the study of this faith, and the enriched understanding of it by leaders of the shrine world. Mr. William P. Woodard, Director of Research for the Institute, served as collaborator and editor of the work. The illustrative sketches were prepared by Sadao Sakamoto, a priest at the Yasukuni Shrine in Tokyo.

The International Institute for the Study of Religions is a non-profit, non-sectarian organization incorporated by the Ministry of Education of the Japanese Government. Its primary purpose is to assist scholars and interested laymen in gaining a better understanding of religions in Japan. To accomplish this purpose the Institute conducts research, promotes lectures and conferences, plans tours, arranges interviews with Japanese scholars and religious leaders, publishes directories, bulletins, and booklets, maintains a reference library on contemporary Japanese religions, and carries on related activities. The Institute also assists Japanese scholars and religious leaders in their study of religions in Japan and abroad.

It has indeed been gratifying to us in the Institute to see the favorable reception enjoyed by this issue of one of its bulletins, and we are pleased that the work is now being published in a revised edition which will receive still wider distribution throughout the world.

Hideo Kishimoto
Director, International Institute
for the Study of Religions

PREFACE

Shinto, the indigenous faith of the Japanese people, has long been a source of fascination for both the casual visitor and old-timer. The strange symbolism, exotic rites, ceremonies, and festivals, and the mystic atmosphere of the shrines constitute a never-ending lure for those who would pry into the recesses of the religious faith of this people. However, except for the student who has the interest, ability, and almost inexhaustible resources in time for his investigation, Shinto remains practically a closed book.

Actually there are very few people, Japanese or foreign, who understand Shinto thoroughly and are able to explain it in detail. These scholars, including the author of this booklet, are the first to admit that there are many things which cannot be clearly explained because in some areas there is still no certain knowledge. To be sure, in the course of the centuries many Japanese have written extensively on Shinto but these are largely expressions of their individual points of view. Except for the relatively short three-quarters of a century of regimentation after the Meiji Restoration, when there was an artificial, government-created authoritative interpretation of Shinto, there has not been any large body of interpretation that is generally accepted.

Free, untrammelled, scientific research in this field is a post-World-War-II phenomenon. Consequently, it is not strange that, relatively speaking, much of it is terra incognita even to many scholars. Today, an increasing number of people are working in the area and it may be that as a result something in the nature of an accepted interpretation will emerge. There are, of course, some excellent scholarly pre-World-War-II books on Shinto, which all who wish to be informed on the subject should read ; but these are all out of print and in some cases very much out of date. There is nothing available that discusses at all adequately the nature and state of Shinto, particularly Shrine Shinto, as it exists in Japan today.

In *The Kami Way,* the International Institute for the Study of Religions has attempted to provide a simple introduction to this subject. Dr. Sokyo Ono, the author, is eminently qualified to do this. As a professor of the great Shinto university, Kokugakuin Daigaku, he is training Shinto priests and scholars and, as a lecturer for the national Association of Shinto Shrines, he is endeavoring to clarify the faith for the active priesthood of the country. Dr. Ono has been a director and loyal supporter of the Institute since its foundation, and the Institute is indebted to him for the careful thought he has given to the preparation of his manuscript.

In *The Kami Way* Dr. Ono out of his rich experience has given the reader a very brief explanation of Shinto shrines and some basic concepts of the kami-faith. Of necessity much that he writes is the expression of his own personal faith. However, in view of his position in the shrine world, it is reasonable to assume that his general position is rather widely accepted. Thus, irrespective of the question of general agreement, the reader will find here an authentic presentation of the kami-faith by one who is deeply immersed in it and is devoting his professional career to its exposition.

In reading *The Kami Way*, some will no doubt feel the explanations are too simple. For them it is unfortunate that a more comprehensive work could not have been published. Others will appreciate the simple, straightforward explanations, but will be confused by what they will regard as a lack of clarity. They may even feel that more questions have been raised than answered. Perhaps most readers will feel this way about the explanation of the kami-concept and chapters four and five which deal with ideological matters. But as Dr. Ono says, " it is impossible to make explicit and clear that which fundamentally by its very nature is vague." (p. 8)

Every possible effort was made to avoid errors. After the original manuscript was translated by Mr. Chido Takeda, who was then a member of the Institute's staff, it was checked and edited by other staff members and parts were re-translated back into Japanese for verification. Finally, before being sent to the press, the revised manuscript was read by a competent Japanese Shinto scholar, whose suggested changes were incorporated.

In regard to the title, the editor must assume full responsibility. In the past *Shinto* has generally been translated as the " Way of the Gods," but to equate the term *kami* with the word " god " is to create a serious misunderstanding. In some cases, Izanagi and Izanami, for example, the kami are as much like people as the gods of Greece and

Rome. In others, such as in the case of the phenomenon of growth, natural objects, the spirit dwelling in trees, and the forces of nature, the term is hardly applicable. Because of this, it is believed that the time has come when the word "kami" should be incorporated into the English language in the same way that Allah, Jehovah, Yahweh and other similar words have been.

In closing, a personal expression of appreciation is due to Dr. Ono not only for his manuscript, but for his patience during long hours of discussion regarding the meaning of certain expressions. The experience has been both pleasant and instructive.

Needless to say, the editor and collaborator is solely responsible for any errors.

William P. Woodard
Director of Research
International Institute for
the Study of Religions

—— NOTE ——

In writing Japanese names the practice of Japanese English-language newspapers is followed: the personal name is written first, then the family name.

神 II 道

THE KAMI WAY

Shinto, the indigenous faith of the Japanese people, is relatively unknown among the religions of the world. Many people are familiar with the *torii*, the typical gateway to Shinto shrines, and some have a vague impression of the unique ornamentation which adorns many shrine roofs. Yet to all but a few, the shrines to which the *torii* leads and the Shinto faith which it symbolizes are very much of an enigma.

Introduction

From time immemorial the Japanese people have believed in and worshipped kami* as an expression of their native racial faith which arose in the mystic days of remote antiquity. To be sure, foreign influences are evident. This kami-faith cannot be fully understood without some reference to them. Yet it is as indigenous as the people that brought the Japanese nation into existence and ushered in its new civilization; and like that civilization, the kami-faith has progressively developed throughout the centuries and still continues to do so in modern times.

Torii

---

* See p. 6

The word *Shintō** (literally, the " Kami Way"), the modern term for this kami-faith, was not current in very primitive times. Nevertheless, it is relatively ancient. The earliest extant Japanese record of its use is in the *Nihon Shoki*** ("Chronicles of Japan,") which was published early in the eighth century. There it was newly employed for the purpose of distinguishing the traditional faith of the people from Buddhism, Confucianism, and Taoism, the continental ways of thinking and believing, which in recent centuries had entered the land. There is no evidence, however, that the term in the sense in which it appears in the *Nihon Shoki* was in general use at that time, either among the people as a whole or among scholars.

Shintō is composed of two ideographs 神 (*shin*), which is equated with the indigenous term *kami*, and 道 (*dō* or *tō*), which is equated with the term *michi*, meaning "way." Originally Chinese (*Shêntao* 神道), in a Confucian context it was used both in the sense of the mystic rules of nature, and to refer to any path leading to a grave. In a Taoist setting, it meant the magical powers peculiar to that faith. In Chinese Buddhist writings there is one instance where Gautama's teachings are called 神道, and another in which the term refers to the concept of the mystic soul. Buddhism in Japan used the word most popularly, however, in the sense of native deities (kami) or the realm of the kami, in which case it meant ghostly beings of a lower order

---

* In this and the next paragraph *Shintō* is being treated as a Japanese word. Elsewhere in the text it is considered an English word and is not italicized.
** See p. 10

than buddhas (*hotoke*). It is generally in this sense that the word was used in Japanese literature subsequent to the *Nihon Shoki*; but about the 13th century, in order to distinguish between it and Buddhism and Confucianism, which had by that time spread throughout the country, the kami-faith was commonly referred to as *Shintō*, a usage which continues to this day.

Unlike Buddhism, Christianity, and Islam, Shinto has neither a founder, such as Gautama the Enlightened One, Jesus the Messiah, or Mohammed the Prophet; nor does it have sacred scriptures, such as the sutras of Buddhism, the Bible, or the Qur'an (Koran).

In its personal aspects " Shinto " implies faith in the kami, usages practiced in accordance with the mind of the kami, and spiritual life attained through the worship of and in communion with the kami. To those who worship kami, "Shinto" is a collective noun denoting all faiths. It is an all-inclusive term embracing the various faiths which are comprehended in the kami-idea. Its usage by Shintoists, therefore, differs from calling Buddha's teaching " Buddhism " and Christ's teaching " Christianity."

In its general aspects Shinto is more than a religious faith. It is an amalgam of attitudes, ideas, and ways of doing things that through two milleniums and more have become an integral part of the *way* of the Japanese people. Thus, Shinto is both a personal faith in the kami and a communal way of life according to the mind of the kami, which emerged in the course of the centuries as various ethnic and cultural influences, both indigenous and foreign, were fused, and the country attained unity under the Imperial Family.

Mythology

The Age of the Kami, the mythological age, sets the Shinto pattern for daily life and worship. In the mythology the names and order of appearance of the kami differ with the various records. According to the *Kojiki** the Kami of the Center of Heaven (Ame-no-minaka-nushi-no-kami) appeared first and then the kami of birth and growth (Taka-mimusubi-no-mikoto and Kami-musubi-no-mikoto). However, it is not until the creative couple, Izanagi-no-mikoto and Izanami-no-mikoto, appear that the mythology really begins. These two, descending from the High Plain of Heaven, gave birth to the Great Eight Islands, that is. Japan, and all things, including many kami. Three of the kami were the most august : the Sun Goddess (Ama-terasu-ō-mikami), the kami of the High Plain of Heaven; her brother (Susa-no-o-no-mikoto), who was in charge of the earth; and the Moon Goddess, (Tsuki-yomi-no-mikoto), who was the kami of the realm of darkness.

The brother, however, according to the *Kojiki*, behaved so very badly and committed so many outrages that the Sun Goddess became angry and hid herself in a celestial cave, which caused the heavens and earth to become darkened. Astonished at this turn of events, the heavenly kami put on an entertainment, including dancing, which brought her out of the cave; and thus light returned to the world. For

* See p. 10

— 4 —

his misdemeanor the brother was banished to the lower world, where by his good behavior he returned to the favor of the other kami, and a descendant of his, the Kami of Izumo (Ōkuni-nushi-no-kami), became a very benevolent kami, who ruled over the Great Eight Islands* and blessed the people. Little is said in the mythology of the Moon Kami.

Subsequently, the grandson of the Sun Goddess, Ninigi-no-mikoto, received instructions to descend and rule Japan. To symbolize his authority he was given three divine treasures : a mirror, a sword, and a string of jewels. Moreover, he was accompanied on his journey by the kami that had participated in the entertainment outside the celestial cave. However, to accomplish his mission it was necessary to negotiate with the Kami of Izumo, who after some discussion agreed to hand over the visible world, while retaining the invisible. At the same time, the Kami of Izumo pledged to protect the heavenly grandson. Ninigi-no-mikoto's great grandson, Emperor Jimmu, became the first human ruler of Japan.

This, in very simple form, is the basic myth which explained for primitive Japanese their origin and the basis of their social structure. It is a description of the evolution of Japanese thought in regard to the origin of life, the birth of the kami and all things out of chaos, the differentiation of all phenomena, and the emergence and evolution of order and harmony. In a sense, the myth amounts to something like a simple constitution for the country. However, in the ancient records the account is not uniform.

---

* See p. 4

There are several versions of a number of events, some of which are contradictory. Thus, the traditions of the various clans were preserved and to a certain extent recognized as valid.

Shinto recognizes today that its beliefs are a continuation of those of this mythological age. In its ritual forms and paraphernalia, this faith fully retains much that is ancient. But just as the Grand Shrine of Ise, which aims at preserving the oldest style of buildings and ancient rituals, has created the most beautiful architectural style in the country today, so Shrine Shinto has outgrown much of its historic mythology. The buds of truth have appeared and have been refined for the people of modern Japan.

Kami

Kami* are the object of worship in Shinto. What is meant by "kami"? Fundamentally, the term is an honorific for noble, sacred spirits, which implies a sense of adoration for their virtues and authority. All beings have such spirits, so in a sense all beings can be called kami or be regarded as potential kami. However, because the term is an honorific, it is not customary to apply it to ordinary individuals

---

* The word *kami* is an indigenous Japanese term which is written with the Chinese character 神. In combination with other characters, this is pronounced *shin* or *jin*. Thus, we have the word "Shintō" 神道, that is, "*Kami* Way," and "*jinja*" 神社, that is, "*kami* dwelling." It is generally customary to translate the ideographs 神 with the words "god" or "deity" in the singular or plural form, and in some cases this is quite correct. However, in this monograph, with a few exceptions it will be left untranslated or be translated with the words "divine" or "sacred." When it is necessary to express a plural concept, such terms as *kami-gami* 神々 and *yaoyorozu no kami* (八百万の神), literally, "eight hundred myriads of *kami*," are used.

or beings. We do not use honorifics in referring to ourselves, or to persons of our own group, whether that group be large or small. Thus, while Shinto teaches that people should be worshipped as kami, they are not in fact usually called *kami*.

Among the objects or phenomena designated from ancient times as kami are the qualities of growth, fertility, and production ; natural phenomena, such as wind and thunder ; natural objects, such as the sun, mountains, rivers, trees and rocks ; some animals ; and ancestral spirits. In the last-named category are the spirits of the Imperial ancestors, the ancestors of noble families, and in a sense all ancestral spirits. Also regarded as kami are the guardian spirits of the land, occupations, and skills; the spirits of national heroes, men of outstanding deeds or virtues, and those who have contributed to civilization, culture, and human welfare ; those who have died for the state or the community ; and the pitiable dead. Not only spirits superior to man, but even some that are regarded as pitiable and weak have nonetheless been considered to be kami.

It is true, that in many instances there are kami which apparently cannot be distinguished from the deities or spirits of animism or animatism, but in modern Shinto all kami are conceived in a refined sense to be spirits with nobility and authority. The kami-concept today includes the idea of justice, order, and divine favor (blessing), and implies the basic principle that the kami function harmoniously in cooperation with one another and rejoice in the evidence of harmony and cooperation in this world.

In Shinto there is no absolute deity that is the creator and ruler of all. The creative function of the world is realized through the harmonious cooperation of the kami in the performance of their respective missions. Even the progenitor of the Imperial Family, the Sun Goddess, the kami who brightens the world with the virtue of the sun and is commonly regarded as the supreme kami of Shinto, consults the opinion of other kami, calls upon them for help, and at times makes concessions to them.

Generally speaking, there is considerable difference between the kami-concept at present and in ancient times. That is, the concept, while remaining in the same basic tradition, has been greatly refined. Nevertheless, the refined and un-refined concepts may still be found side by side.

There are many points about the kami-concept that cannot be fully understood, and there is some disagreement even among modern scholars on this subject. The Japanese people themselves do not have a clear idea regarding the kami. They are aware of the kami intuitively at the depth of their consciousness and communicate with the kami directly without having formed the kami-idea conceptually or theologically. Therefore, it is impossible to make explicit and clear that which fundamentally by its very nature is vague. Only in recent times have Shinto leaders been en-deavoring to develop a unified theology regarding the kami. Thus although increasing attention is being paid to this subject, there are still many matters that are not clear even among Shintoists.

Guardian Kami

Each kami may be said to have its own special characteristics, capacity, and mission; and in a sense each is worshipped as the founder or guardian of some definite object
or phenomenon. For example, one is concerned with the
distribution of water, another with the manufacture of
medicine, and still another with the healing process. Then
there are ancestral kami that are the protectors of a given
group, and those that are the patrons of a given territory
or of clans, that is, social groups based on kinship. It is
quite proper to ask what almost any kami protects, but a
clear answer cannot always be given.

Prominent among the kami are the guardians of the clans
(*uji*). These are generally called *ujigami*, and are always
worshipped in shrines. Throughout the country there are
many shrines of this origin. But with the increasing mobility
of the people and the gradual break-up of the clans the term
ujigami was also applied to the guardians of the residents
of a given area as well as the area itself. Thus, while in
the past lineal descent was a primary factor, today the common community relationship has come to assume greater
importance. Nevertheless, in many cases the consciousness
of lineal descent from a clan is still strong and some persons
regularly return to their native places to take part in the
festivals of their guardian kami.

Scriptures

Shinto does not possess sacred scriptures, such as are found in many other religions, — a fact which is a significant indication of the character of the Shinto faith itself. Nevertheless, there are certain ancient records that are regarded as authoritative and provide its historical as well as its spiritual basis.

The earliest of these were compiled by Imperial order and contain the mythology and early history of the Japanese people. The *Kojiki* ("Record of Ancient Matters") is the oldest extant Japanese historical record. Its date is 712 of the Christian era. It provides an account of events down to the year 628. Though written in Chinese ideographs the style is ancient, pure Japanese and through it we can know something of the style of the earlier oral transmission from generation to generation. Consequently it is especially valued. The *Nihongi* or *Nihon Shoki* ("Chronicles of Japan"), which appeared eight years later and brings the record down to the year 697, was written in Chinese and thus changed the form of transmission. However, it is more detailed than the *Kojiki*; and because several mythologies or versions are given of some events, it has a special value in matters in which the *Kojiki* is lacking.

These two documents are especially highly regarded by Shintoists. They contain the only extant ancient records of the Imperial Family and of the several clans which formed the Japanese nation. Their purpose was to make clear the origin of the Imperial Throne, clan lineage, and other matters which constitute the basis of Japanese society and customs. They are, nonetheless, rich in information regarding ancient Shinto rituals and practices, and the established functions and inviolable rights of the several clans in relation to the state cult. They are an expression of the claims of the respective clans in relation to Japan's social structure, and are of such a nature that without them disintegration of the clan system would have been almost inevitable.

The *Kujiki* ("Chronicle of Ancient Events"), *Kogoshui* ("Gleanings from Ancient Stories") and *Engi Shiki* ("Detailed Laws of the Engi Period") are also primary sources of information. The *Kujiki* claims to have been first written about the year 620, or one hundred years before the *Nihongi*, but the extant version is almost certainly a forgery. Nevertheless, it is very ancient and is of some value even though it contains much that is also found in the *Kojiki* and *Nihongi*. Unfortunately, it has not been translated. The *Kogoshui* was written in 807 and adds somewhat to our information about early Shinto. The *Engi Shiki* was published in 927 and is the principal source of information on early Shinto, ceremonial prayers, rituals, and the manner of administering divine affairs.

It must be stressed, however, that none of these writings are regarded as holy writ in the sense that the term is used in Christianity and Islam. They are primarily historical records which, in addition to their political or dynastic interest, embody the ancient forms of the kami-faith.

Shinto did not develop a canon because, in the first place, the shrine and its ritual mediated the kami-faith to the people ; and in the second place, the acceptance of the shrine as the symbol of their communal faith made it unnecessary to guide the people by means of doctrine and instruction. In the course of history very few people have evaded their communal obligation with respect to Shrine worship.

To be sure, there have been times in the past when, due to the confrontation of foreign faiths and the threatened collapse of traditions, the development of a canon seemed essential; but in no case did conditions actually become very serious, so no continuous effort has been made to establish one. The social changes and confusion of thought which exist today confront Shrine Shinto with a new situation that appears to call for the development of something that will serve as a means of maintaining and deepening Shrine Shinto faith. As yet, however, there is no clear indication as to how this can be accomplished.

Types of Shinto

Popular Shinto There are several types of Shinto. The least tangible is Popular Shinto. Kami-worship is deeply rooted in the everyday life of the people. Many of the ideas and customs associated with it in primitive times have been preserved through the centuries in unorganized folkways. These, along with much that is of foreign origin, are called "Folk Shinto" or "Popular Faith."

Domestic Shinto Domestic Shinto, refers to the religious practices centering in the Shinto home altar. This is described briefly in Chapter III under "Worship in the Home."

Sectarian Shinto Sectarian Shinto is composed of a number of heterogeneous groups which the Meiji government, in connection with the nationalization of shrines and the emphasis on shrine worship as a state cult, placed under the supervision of a separate government office. Subsequently, most of the principal groups became independent religious bodies and were officially classified as "Sectarian Shinto." There were thirteen such sects in pre-war days.

Imperial Household Shinto Imperial Household Shinto is the name given to the religious rites conducted at the three shrines within the palace grounds, which are exclusively for the use of the Imperial Family, and to certain related matters. The central shrine (Kashiko-dokoro), which is dedicated to the mythological ancestress of the Imperial Family, goes back for its origin to the descent of Ninigi-no-mikoto, the grandson of the Sun Goddess to whom the sacred mirror (Yata-no-kagami) was given. After being kept in the palace for some centuries, a replica was made that was enshrined in the Kashiko-dokoro and the sacred symbol itself was enshrined at the Inner Shrine (Naiku) of Ise. This mirror is symbolic of the spirit of the Sun Goddess and is one of the three articles of the Imperial Regalia, handed down by the emperors from generation to generation. On the west side of the central shrine is the Ancestral Spirits Sanctuary (Kōrei-den) which, as the name implies, enshrines the divine spirits of the successive emperors. On the east side is the Sanctuary of the Kami (Shin-den), which is sacred to all the kami of heaven and earth.

In ancient times responsibility for the Shinto ceremonies conducted at the court was in the hands of the Nakatomi and Imbe families, who handed down to their respective descendants the traditional procedures that each performed. Today, the hereditary system no longer exists ; but the ceremonies conducted at the palace shrines are almost the same as the rites provided for in the Imperial Ceremonies Law of 1908. The ritualists, officials of the Imperial Household, conduct some of the ceremonies, but at the most important ceremonies the Emperor himself, in accordance with ancient tradition, leads the official ritualists in the rites. In April, 1959, these sanctuaries came to the public notice when the wedding of H. I. H. the Crown Prince was conducted there. A phase of Imperial Household Shinto is the practice of sending Imperial messengers to make offerings at certain shrines and mausolea which have a special connection with the Imperial Family.

Shrine Shinto The oldest and most prevalent type of the kami-faith is Shrine Shinto. Shrines date from very earliest times. There were shrines even before the dawn of Japanese history. During the course of the centuries, as the clans expanded throughout the length and breadth of the land, the number of shrines gradually increased until at the beginning of the twentieth century there were nearly two hundred thousand. After the Meiji Restoration they were nationalized, organized into what became known as the " Shrine System," and later were gradually reduced to about one hundred ten thousand. At the end of World War II shrines were disestablished and became private institutions. There are approximately eighty thousand today.

— 14 —

The Grand Shrine of Ise   The Grand Shrine of Ise is unique among the shrines of the country and deserves special mention. Its principal deity, the Sun Goddess, was originally the tutelary kami of the Yamato clan from which emerged the Imperial Family that has ruled Japan throughout its history. With the ascendancy of the Yamato clan to suzerainty over the entire country, the shrine became in a sense the tutelary shrine of the nation. The Grand Shrine of Ise is generally regarded as standing at the apex of all shrines. Worship there is more than an expression of faith in the enshrined kami. It is the highest expression of respect to the Emperor and to all that is best in the culture, history, and racial consciousness of the Japanese people.

State Shinto   Imperial Household Shinto and Shrine Shinto, along with certain well-defined ideas regarding Japanese origins and history, constituted what was formerly known as " State Shinto." This ceased to exist when the shrines were disestablished.

Organization

From the dawn of history until the Meiji Restoration, with the exception of a few that were closely related to the Imperial Family, the shrines were primarily communal institutions. Then for a period of approximately seventy years, they were state institutions under the supervision of the national government. Finally, as a result of the Shinto Directive issued by the Supreme Commander for the Allied

Powers on December 15, 1945, they were disestablished and became private institutions.

The Directive was nothing short of revolutionary. It confronted shrines with a totally novel and extremely difficult situation. Historically, a few shrines had been closely connected with the Imperial Family, and some had been in the hands of the nobility, but for the most part they were either held by the common people or had something of a dual status. Regardless of this, however, with a few notable exceptions all the shrines had been closely connected with the common people. Even though they received gifts of land and money from the central government, the nobility, feudal lords, or influential families, the position and authority of the traditional priesthood and the responsibility of the local parishioners for the performance of rites and festivals were usually respected.

At the time of the Meiji Restoration this situation was greatly changed. Shrines were made state institutions and the priests became government officials. However, control and supervision was very strict only in respect to the two hundred twenty-four shrines (*kankoku-heisha*) supervised by the national government: yet in the last analysis all shrines were subject to the decisions of the appropriate government offices and dependent on them in all important matters relative to personnel, property, rites, and festivals. This situation prevailed for about three-quarters of a century.

Prior to the Shinto Directive there were three national organizations which in a general way were concerned with Shrine Shinto. These were the National Association of

Shrine Priests (Jingi Kai), the Research Institute for the Japanese Classics (Kōten Kōkyū Sho), and the Grand Shrine Supporters Association (Jingū Hōsai Kai). But affiliation was on an individual basis and the organizations themselves had nothing to do directly with shrine administration or shrine activities. As for the individual shrines, there was no connection whatsoever between them, not even among those in a given geographical area or those that had the same objects of worship.

Consequently, when the Directive suddenly removed government control and supervision, no one had any idea about what should be done. The pertinent section of the Directive prohibited forthwith the " sponsorship, support, perpetuation, control and dissemination of Shinto " by any government agency or employee acting in an official capacity, but it contained no provisions regarding any subsequent reorganization of the shrines and there were no suggestions by Occupation authorities as to what should be done. Thus, each of the hundred thousand and more shrines was temporarily completely stranded without any organic or connectional relations whatsoever, and with no recognized leadership. The priests, of course, lost their official status and became private individuals.

By February 3, 1946, however, the above-mentioned national organizations had dissolved and the leaders had established a new comprehensive body, called the Association of Shinto Shrines (Jinja Honchō), which invited local shrines throughout the country to affiliate. All but a few agreed to do so. About 1,000 remained independent and some 250 formed small associations, primarily geographical in scope, such as the Southern Hokkaido Shrine Association (Hokkaidō Jinja Kyōkai), the Shrine Association (Jinja Honkyō) of Kyoto, and the Kiso Mitake Shrine Association (Kiso Mitake Honkyō) in Nagano Prefecture. Of those that have remained entirely independent, only sixteen are large, important shrines which were formerly under the control of the national government. Thus, it can be seen that the shrines succeeded better than some other religious organizations in maintaining their unity in the post-World-War-II period.

The Association of Shinto Shrines is under the administration of a board of councillors, composed of representatives from forty-six prefectural associations (Jinja-chō), which selects an executive secretary and is responsible for all major policy decisions. There are six departments in the headquarters which carry on activities appropriate to their names: secretariat, finance, general administration, teaching (*kyō-gaku*), investigation, and mutual aid. The headquarters of the Association is located at Wakagi-chō, Shibuya-ku in Tokyo. The late Honorable Nobusuke Takatsukasa, chief priest of Meiji Shrine, was the first President. Yukitada Sasaki, former chief priest of the Grand Shrine of Ise, is his successor. Madame Fusako Kitashirakawa, the High Priestess of Ise, is the Honorary President. As of June, 1958, a total of 79,457 shrines were affiliated with the Association. This is not the number of separate shrines, but the number that are incorporated. In some cases one incorporated body includes several shrines.

On the local level the shrines are managed by the priests

and committees composed of representatives of the worshippers. They are usually incorporated as religious juridical persons. They own their land and buildings, and raise funds for their own support through private gifts and offerings.

The Association is closely connected with the Kokugakuin University, the only Shinto institution of higher education in Japan. It is also affiliated with the Religions League of Japan (Nihon Shūkyō Renmei). The *Jinja Shinpō* ("Shrine News"), an independent weekly publication, is more or less the unofficial spokesman for the Shrine Shinto world.

Typical Approach to a Shrine

神 **II** 道

SHRINES

Shrines and Shrine Paraphernalia

Shrines are a spontaneous manifestation of the people's faith in the kami, and shrine rites and festivals are the highest expression of that faith.

Originally the kami-rites were performed at significant places, particularly those where a manifestation of some kami was first observed or experienced, regardless of the convenience of the site. As the population increased and civilization became more complex, structures were erected which were usually more readily accessible. In some cases these were only worship halls, such as may be seen today at the Ōmiwa Shrine in Yamato, Nara Prefecture, which considers Mount Miwa itself to be the dwelling of the kami. In most cases, however, sanctuaries were constructed with inner chambers where the kami were regarded as symbolically present at all times.

Divine Dwellings The primary purpose of a shrine is to provide a dwelling place for one or more kami and a place where the kami can be served, that is, worshipped in accordance with Shinto beliefs and practices. Shrines are not

PLATE 2. MEIJI SHRINE, TOKYO. Dedicated to the Emperor Meiji (1867-1912), the roofs of this shrine are fine examples of the Nagare, or flowing style.

PLATE 3. MEIJI SHRINE, TOKYO. Worshippers throng the shrine precincts on New Year's Day.

erected in order to propagate the faith nor to teach doctrine, although both are regarded as important.

Divine Symbols   Symbolic of the kami's presence is a sacred object, called the " divine body " (*shintai*) or " august-spirit-substitute " (*mitamashiro*). This object is housed within the innermost chamber of the shrine sanctuary. When the sacred symbol is present, the inner sanctuary is inviolable. And, since the building itself, as well as the precincts and auxiliary structures, partakes in some measure of the sanctity of the kami, they are considered objects worthy of great respect, if not worship. It is the presence of the symbol that makes a building a sanctuary. If the symbol is removed, the religious meaning of the area ceases to exist.

Sanctuary Plan   Except for a few unusual cases such as the Ōmiwa Shrine, mentioned above, and the Grand Shrine of Izumo, in its simplest form and irrespective of size, a shrine generally consists of an inner compartment, a holy of holies, for the sacred symbol, and a space in front for offerings either within or without the structure. As the sanctuary increases in size, the interior may become both more spacious and more elaborate, but the basic arrangement of an inner sanctuary and a place in front for offerings remains unchanged.

Two swinging doors at the front of the inner compartment, which are always kept closed and locked except during special rites, protect the sacred symbol from being violated. Even when the doors are opened, a curtain of split bamboo or some other material hangs in the entrance-way and prevents the priest and worshippers alike from looking within. Before this inner compartment are set tables upon which offerings are placed. At either side, there are sometimes banners and human or animal images. Seated human figures with bows and arrows and dressed in ancient court costumes, Korean dogs (*Koma Inu*) and similar images are usual in the larger shrines. Ordinarily, in a central position on the offering table or behind it, there is at least one perpendicular wand from the top of which, suspended on either side, is some flat paper, usually white, folded in a unique style. At one side is a purification wand, also placed perpendicular in a stand, from which hang white strips of paper and flax streamers. Not infrequently there is a mirror in the center between the offering table and the doors to the inner chamber. This mirror has a symbolic meaning, but is not an object of worship. There may be exceptions but, as a rule, pictures are not hung on shrine walls. Framed ideographs drawn by some famous scholar, calligrapher, or well-known person are frequently found hanging above the entrance to a shrine or on an inner transom.

Before the sanctuary stands an offering box. Directly above it may hang a bell to which a rope is attached; but a great many shrines do not have bells.

A shrine which is devoted to the worship of more than one kami may have an equal number of separate inner compartments, each of which has its own sacred symbol. In this case, there is usually one principal and one or more subordinate kami. In not a few cases an enshrined kami has a plural nature.

Mirrors The mirror is one of the most common symbols of Shinto. In a shrine it may be a sacred object of worship, in which case it is within the inner compartment and is never visible to either priest or worshipper. Or it may be an ornament. As an ornament it is always placed directly in front of the doors to the inner compartment.

A mirror has a clean light that reflects everything as it is. It symbolizes the stainless mind of the kami, and at the same time is regarded as a sacred symbolic embodiment of the fidelity of the worshipper towards the kami.

In mythology the mirror is a mysterious object. In ancient society it was an object of ceremonial and religious significance rather than of daily use. In order to catch her spirit, a mirror was hung outside the cave where the Sun Goddess hid. Ninigi-no-mikoto was told by the Sun Goddess "to honor and worship the mirror" as "her spirit."

Teachings about the significance of the mirror vary. The *Jinnō Shōtōki* (1339) by Chikafusa Kitabatake states that

> the mirror hides nothing. It shines without a selfish mind. Everything good and bad, right and wrong, is reflected without fail. The mirror is the source of honesty because it has the virtue of responding according to the shape of objects. It points out the fairness and impartiality of the divine will.

The mirror is the sacred symbol at the Grand Shrine of Ise as well as at many other shrines. The mirror that stands before the inner sanctuary at Yasukuni Shrine in Tokyo is an ornament, which is especially valued because it was a gift from Emperor Meiji.

Symbolic Offering The *Gohei*, which consists of a wand with strips of paper folded in a zigzag fashion hanging at either side and stands in a central position before the doors of the inner chamber, is a symbolic offering and at the same time indicates the presence of the kami in the sanctuary. Usually there is only one *gohei*

Gohei

and the paper is white; but in some shrines there are several, one for each enshrined kami. The paper is sometimes gold, silver, red, or dark blue, and not infrequently metal or cloth is used instead of paper. This wand with paper inserted into the split end is believed to be a relic of the time when cloth was presented in this manner at shrines as an offering.

Purification Wand The wand(*Harai-gushi*), which has many long paper streamers and a few strands of flax, is for the rite of purification. In performing this rite the wand is removed from its stand by a priest who, facing the worshipper or object to be purified, waves it first over his left, then the right, and finally back to the left shoulder with a characteristic flourish before replacing it.

Haraigushi
Purification Wand

Sometimes a small branch of the sacred *sakaki* tree is used instead of this wand.

Banners Banners symbolize the presence of the kami and are at the same time offerings to the kami. Some banners of Chinese style have figures of the sun, moon, clouds, or possibly animals. These presumably express the idea that the kami are heavenly beings which provide protection. Some banners have the same origin as the *gohei*. Generally speaking, however, the banners are probably ornamental rather than symbolic, and merely add dignity to the shrine.

Sword, Halberd and Shield The sword and jewels, which are enclosed in brocade and are hung from the banner standards, as well as the halberd and shield, symbolize both the power to defend the kami from evil and the power of the kami to protect justice and peace: Some understand the mirror, jewel, and sword to symbolize the virtues of wisdom, benevolence, and courage respectively.

Sacred Rope Straw rope (*shimenawa*) from which depend short strips of zigzag-cut paper may be seen stretched between the pillars at the entrance to shrines as well as

Shimenawa
Sacred rope with paper and flax pendants

elsewhere, both within and without the main buildings. These ropes are used to symbolically indicate sacred places where kami are believed to dwell or objects offered to the kami. They are also sometimes used in ordinary buildings during the New Year's season, at festival times, and on special occasions. There are various types, some of which are unique with certain shrines, as for example, the extremely heavy tapering rope at the Grand Shrine of Izumo. However, the shape has no special religious significance.

Shrine Buildings and Compounds

A shrine may consist of a single sanctuary or a group of sanctuaries with numerous auxiliary buildings located either within a single precinct or in one or more detached precincts. Small, single-structure shrines are most numerous; but the typical shrine compound has an oratory, which stands directly in front of the main sanctuary, an ablution pavilion, and several auxiliary buildings. Sometimes there is an offering hall and a place for reciting prayers between the main sanctuary and the oratory, but under a common or connecting roof. A sacred place to prepare food offerings is always essential. Among the most common auxiliary buildings are subordinate shrines, a shrine office, a place to prepare offerings, a hall for sacred dances, and a pavilion for picture votive offerings. Other buildings often found at the large shrines include a ceremonial hall, the priests' quarters, a sacred stable, a storehouse for the sacred palanquin, a treasure house, and a theater for Noh plays. Within the compound there may be also a *sumō* arena, a sacred bridge, memorial tablets, and stone or metal lanterns. Statues are relatively rare. Occasionally there is burial ground adjoining a shrine compound, that is usually for the war-dead, who are venerated at the shrine, or for former priests and their families. Generally, however, there are no burial grounds near shrines.

Shrine compounds vary considerably both in their layout and the number of buildings. Some cover only small areas, others constitute large tracts of land, such as, for example, the Kirishima Shrine which covers several thousand acres. When the contour of the land does not determine the lines, the area is usually rectangular in shape.

Location The location of a shrine is not merely a matter of finding a vacant piece of land. As a general rule shrines are related in some manner to their natural surroundings. They are in a given location because of some special tree, grove, rock, cave, mountain, river, or the seashore, for example; or because of a close relationship with an ancient family, perhaps the pioneer that opened up the area. Not infrequently in rural communities shrines are so completely concealed in dense groves or forests that only the local residents are aware of their existence.

All too often in downtown metropolitan areas shrines have been forced by circumstances beyond their control to give up the original natural beauty of their surroundings and be satisfied with an almost barren site totally devoid of foliage. This is ordinarily the result of population pressures which have transformed a relatively secluded site into a throbbing commercial or industrial center. In some cases, of course, the location is due merely to the availability of the site, and without any meaningful ties either to the land or to the vicinity.

In every case, however, once a kami has been enshrined, the precincts, like the shrine itself, acquire a special sanctity ; and every effort is made, when the surroundings themselves are not naturally beautiful or impressive, to create a beauty which will instill in the minds of the worshippers a mystic sense of closeness to the unseen divine world and to nature. The natural beauty imparts to the worshipper a religious impetus to move from the mundane to the higher and deeper divine world, which can transform his life into one of closer fellowship with the kami.

Walls A fence or wall often surrounds the compound in order to protect it from desecration. In the case of large shrines, there may also be a second one, which encloses a smaller inner area, and finally a third which surrounds the inner sanctuary and worship hall.

Torii With rare exceptions the entrance to shrines, other than small wayside shrines, is marked by one or more *torii*, the gateway which symbolically marks off the mundane world from the world of the kami, the secular from the spiritual. The origin of the gateway, which may or may not have come from the Asiatic mainland, and the reason for writing the word with the characters meaning " bird " (鳥 *tori*) and " to be " (居 i), that is, "bird perch," need not detain us here.

The origin is obscure and has no particular relevance to its present use.

In ancient Japan the *torii* was in common use as a gateway but in the course of time it was limited to Shinto sanctuaries, Imperial mausolea, and a few graves. Occasionally, a *torii* will be found at the foot of trees or beside a rock or well.

In 1884 public use of the *torii* was officially restricted by law to only state shrines and certain sanctuaries of the Shūsei and Taisei sects of Shinto, which at the time were using it as a gateway. Today, even though this restriction is not in force, the *torii* continues to be seen only at Shinto shrines, a few sanctuaries of the above-named sects, at the entrance to Imperial mausolea, and in connection with some graves. When found at the entrance to or within a Buddhist temple compound, other than a burial ground, there is almost certain to be a shrine of some sort nearby, often at the summit of a miniature mountain.

Some shrines encourage the devout to present *torii* as votive offerings. These are frequently erected close together along the approach to the main or a subordinate sanctuary so as to form an archway. Inari shrines, notably Fushimi Inari south of Kyoto, are famous for these picturesque approaches.

In a relatively few cases a *torii* may stand astride a public thoroughfare. One of the best known of these is in front of the Heian Shrine in Kyoto. In some instances, such as the Tsurugaoka Hachiman Shrine in Kamakura, there may be a long approach outside the shrine compound itself on which stand several *torii*. Such symbolic gateways remind the people of the presence of the kami in the community. At one time such approaches were probably considered as a part of the shrine compound.

Ryōbu Torii   Kasuga Torii   Myōjin Torii

Originally, the *torii* was of very simple construction. It consisted of unfinished wooden pillars and two crossbeams in characteristic proportions. Later the pillars and beams were planed but unpainted. Then, due to continental influence, they were painted and became more complicated in structure until in some cases, such as the magnificent lacquered red *torii* which stands in the water at Miyajima before the Itsukushima Shrine, they became very ornate.

Torii are generally made of timber, but in modern times stone and metal have been substituted and of late some have been made of concrete. There are more than twenty different types of *torii*, most of which are named from the shrines with which they are associated. For example, there is an Ise *torii*, a Hachiman *torii* from the Iwashimizu Hachiman Shrine, and a Miwa *torii* from the Ōmiwa Shrine.

Other Gates In addition to *torii*, many large shrines have gates which can be closed at night. Some of these are very imposing. Two types prevail. Those constructed after the separation of Buddhism and Shinto, having unpainted timbers and a thatched, tiled, or copper roof, such as those at Yasukuni and Meiji shrines in Tokyo, are generally in the style of "pure" Shinto. A second type usually consists of a massive, somewhat ornate, red or black-lacquered two-storey structure with enclosures on either side which house two or sometimes four images. The enclosures are often protected by wire meshing to prevent the images from being injured or defaced. This style was introduced during the period when Buddhism generally dominated the shrine world. The magnificent Yōmeimon at the Tōshōgū in Nikkō is the example par excellence of this style. The gates at the Yasaka (Gion) Shrine and Kamo shrines in Kyoto, and the Hakozaki Shrine in Fukuoka are also good examples. In a few exceptional cases there are gates which are very unusual. Such is the Suiten-mon of the Akama Shrine in Yamaguchi Prefecture and the gate of the Oyama Shrine in Kanazawa City, which was designed by a Dutch engineer.

The Approach A road or path leading to a shrine is called "the approach" (*sandō*). Technically speaking the approach is the path leading from the first *toru* to the oratory or sanctuary, but in common parlance even public roads which lead to a shrine may be so designated. This is especially the case when one or more *torii* stand on public roads; but even when there are no *torii*, the term is sometimes applied. Thus, in Tokyo the broad highway leading to Meiji Shrine is called the "main approach" (*omote sandō*), while the other two roads are called the "west approach" and "east approach," respectively.

Within the compound the approach is often a dirt road or path on the surface of which small stones or pebbles have been spread. In some cases the entire area in front of a shrine may be covered with neatly-raked gravel or fine sand. This is done to maintain a harmonious natural atmosphere and creates a pure, pleasant feeling in the mind of the worshippers.

If the traditional pattern is followed, the approach turns somewhere between the first *torii* and the oratory or sanctuary. However, as conditions do not always permit a strict observance of this tradition, direct approaches are common.

Guardians of the Gate and Precincts   The precincts are symbolically protected in several ways from evil spirits and misfortune. Sometimes in front and on either side of the entrance there are miniature shrines that are guardians of the entrance. Then, if there is a large gate, within the enclosure on either side may be found two rather ferocious-looking beings with semi-human features and of more than human dimensions. These Deva kings (*Niō-sama*) are of Indian origin and more commonly are found in the gates of Buddhist temples. They are actually kindly in nature, their ferocious countenance being a means of warding off evil spirits. Also within these enclosures, sometimes facing the shrine and sometimes facing outward, are two austere dignitaries in a sitting position, dressed in ancient court costumes with a sheathed sword at the belt and arrows in a holder on their backs, while in their hands they hold bows. These figures represent two mythological kami and are likewise traditional guardians.

Guardian Lions

Animal images constitute a third type of symbolic protectors. These are in pairs, male and female, and ordinarily stand on pedestals on either side near the first *torii* or along the approach. They may also be placed on either side of the approach directly in front of the sanctuary or even within the sanctuary itself. The most common types of guardian animals are images of dogs and lions.

Finally, there is sometimes a guardian kami of the land that is housed in a sanctuary within the precinct.

At Inari shrines, where fox images are found, and at Kasuga shrines, where there are deer, the animals are believed to be the attendants or messengers of the kami, rather than guardians. The messenger of the Mitsumine Shrine is a wolf, and that of Hie Shrine is a monkey. An image of a horse, is a symbolic mount for the kami.

Lanterns, Memorial Tablets, and Statues On either side of the approach, both within and outside the shrine compound, are frequently found stone or bronze lanterns. The lanterns as a rule are gifts from devout parishioners, either individually or as associations. The idea of giving lanterns, which have the utilitarian value of marking the approach, may have originated from the custom of making fires in order to greet and honor the kami. Occasionally, there are statues of local heroes or some personages connected with the local community. More often there are memorial tablets, also the gifts of devout parishioners, that recall some significant local or national historic event. Not infrequently one finds along the approach a stone pillar, a "hundred-times stone" (*hyakudo ishi*), as it is called, which marks the place from which worshippers walk back and forth to the sanctuary or oratory in order to more earnestly seek the fulfillment of a prayer. In some cases there are devices, such as small tabs on a cord, for counting the number of times.

Ablution Pavilion Somewhere along the approach, probably not very far from the oratory, is an ablution pavilion (*temizuya*) for ceremonial purification by means of rinsing the mouth and pouring water over the finger tips. This symbolic cleansing is considered indispensable as a preparation for worship and no shrine fails to provide some such facility. Usually there is a simple open pavilion with a stone basin filled with clear water and one or more wooden dippers. With this rite evil and pollution are ceremonially removed and the worshipper becomes once again pure. Originally purification was performed at a spring or stream, as at the Inner Shrine at Ise, for example, or by the seashore, and this is still considered somewhat ideal.

List of Donors Sometimes seen at the entrance or along the approach are rough, unsightly, wooden frames, with wooden slabs on which are written sums of money and the names of individuals. This constitutes a list of those who have contributed to some special project of the shrine, such as repairs or reconstruction. The normal gifts made periodically at festival time or in connection with some special service are not posted in this manner.

Sacred Trees Not infrequently there is one tree in a compound that is within an enclosure and about which hangs a straw rope with short paper streamers (*shimenawa*). This is often a very large and old tree, and is regarded as uniquely sacred. In addition there may also be one or more *sakaki* (*Cleyera ochnacca*) trees, an evergreen, which is the sacred tree of Shinto.

Shrine Stalls Either in connection with the shrine office or in a small separate structure there will be a place to secure charms, amulets, postcards and articles used in connection with worship in the home. Technically these things are not for sale but are given in return for a small offering.

Architecture

Shrine architecture manifests considerable variety of style, which in most cases reflects the age and to some extent the place in which certain shrines arose and sometimes the historical periods through which they have passed. Many shrine structures show the effect of continental influence, but there are two relatively pure Japanese types, that are very ancient and are generally considered to be typical of Shinto. One is the Shinmei, literally, " divine-brightness " style which is best represented by the Grand Shrine of Ise. This type is also known as the Tenchi Kongen, literally, " heaven-earth origin " style. The other is the Taisha style, which is typified by the Grand Shrine of Izumo.

Traditionally shrines have been constructed of cypress and thatched with miscanthus or cypress bark. Today, however, because of the increased fire hazard, reinforced concrete is frequently used in cities and roofs covered with tile or copper are common. In rare cases stone shrines are to be found. Paint and ornamentation are an indication of continental influence.

Roof Ornamentation

Among the characteristic features of shrine architecture, the ornamentation of the roof with *chigi* and *katsuogi* is the most unique and striking to foreign visitors. For the shrine worshipper these add a peculiarly mystic quality to the atmosphere. The *chigi* were originally formed by an extension of the end beams of the roof which cross at both ends of the ridge and continue upward at an angle for several feet. The short logs, which are now made of finished wood and taper at each end, are called *katsuogi*, because of their resemblance to the shape of the dried fish (*katsuo-bushi*)

PLATE 4. GRAND SHRINE OF ISE: INNER SHRINE. An example of the Shinmei type of shrine structure. Shinmei (literally "divine brightness") is a relatively pure Japanese style in shrine architecture.

PLATE 5. GRAND SHRINE OF ISE: GATE OF INNER SHRINE. A *torii*, the gateway which symbolically marks off the mundane world from the world of the kami, guards the way to the inner precincts.

PLATE 6. GRAND SHRINE OF ISE: OUTER SHRINE. Walls enclose inner and outer compounds of shrines. Precincts, as well as shrine, acquire a special sanctity.

PLATE 7. GRAND SHRINE OF ISE: OUTER SHRINE. At a ceremonial service white-robed priests are garbed in the style of Heian period.

used in Japanese cooking. Usually there are three, five, or seven *katsuogi*; but the Inner Shrine at Ise has ten and the Outer Shrine nine. Originally a structural necessity in order to hold the roof down and in place, in later times the *chigi* and *katsuogi* became purely decorative and today are rarely seen except on shrines. Both are thought of as symbols of Shrine Shinto, yet many shrines do not have them, and only the *chigi* are mentioned in the ritual prayers and other ceremonial documents.

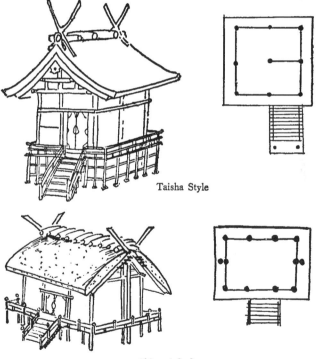

Taisha Style

Shinmei Style

In addition to the Shinmei and Taisha styles mentioned above, there are a number of other styles which are designated by the names of well-known representative shrines (Ōtori, Sumiyoshi, Kasuga, Hachiman, Hiyoshi, Gion, Kibitsu and Sengen). A few have descriptive names, such as *Gongen* (Incarnation) and *Nagare* (Flowing). Generally, shrines having the same name, Kasuga shrines, for example, adopt the style of architecture of the original shrine bearing that name. Thus examples of the various kinds of architecture may be found in many parts of the country.

Only a very few shrines are distinctly unique in their construction. The two shrines at Ise are, of course, among these, but the two-storied sanctuary of Fuji Sengen in Fuji-nomiya, Shizuoka Prefecture, is almost without parallel, and the same is true of the Kibitsu Shrine in Okayama Prefecture, that is noted for its large sanctuary which measures 62.4 feet by 49.8 feet. Except for the Shinmei, Taisha, Ōtori, and Sumiyoshi styles, foreign influence is very noticeable in all those mentioned above. All are painted, most of them in red. The Kasuga style is unique for its curved *chigi*. The Nagare style, the finest examples of which can be seen in the very modern Meiji Shrine in Tokyo, can be recognized by the flowing lines of the roof which extends down in front over a stairway. The Irimoya style has a roof that is gabled in the upper part and hipped or sloping in the lower part. Kashiwara Shrine, dedicated to the veneration of Jimmu Tennō, the first emperor, is an outstanding example of this style.

Generally speaking the changing styles of shrine architecture appear to reflect the development from century to century of Buddhist temples, castles and Japanese dwellings, especially those of the upper classes. From a simple, single-frame structure the houses were gradually enlarged and as more rooms were brought under one roof or closely connected by adjacent roofs, the external features changed accordingly. The Irimoya style, for example, was at first used by the nobility and later adopted by shrines. The same is true of

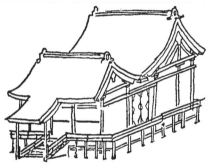 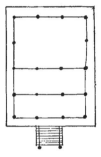

Hachiman Style

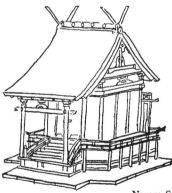 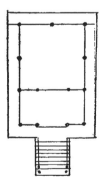

Nagare Style

the much broader Gion style. The Gongen style, which is most gorgeously represented by the Tōshōgu of Nikkō, and the Yatsumune (Eight Roof) style, typified by the Kitano Shrine in Kyoto, notably reveal the influence of Buddhism on shrine construction.

Priests and Shrine Functionaries

Shrines are served by priests, who are primarily ritualists. In very primitive society there appear to have been no priestly orders. The observance of communal rites and ceremonies was the responsibility of all the people. However, there were shaman, frequently women, who were thought to possess special occult power which enabled them, by observing the ritualistic requirements for purification, to achieve a position of prestige

Priest

and respect in the community and to function as mediums for contact with the kami. These shaman performed many of the local rites. Later, on the clan level, the heads of the clans or local families performed the most important rituals on behalf of their people, while other ceremonies were conducted by minor officials or specifically designated individuals. In time, these functions became the prerogative of certain families and a hereditary local priesthood emerged.

About the middle of the first millenium, according to Occidental chronology, four priestly classes had authority at

the court. These were the ritualists, mainly from the Nakatomi family, who had charge of ceremonies and read the
official ritual prayers; the abstainers, the Imbe family, that
maintained ceremonial purity in order to ward off pollution
and keep constant contact with the kami; the diviners, the
Urabe family, that was responsible for learning the will of
the kami; and the dancers and musicians (*sarume*). Except
for a few very important priestly rites, which were performed by the Emperor personally, these priestly classes
were responsible for the rituals both at the court and at
shrines closely related to the Imperial Family.

The administration of state ceremonies and control of the
local priesthood in the eighth century was vested in the
head of an Office of Divine Affairs (*Jingi Kan*), which occupied a position above the cabinet. Except for the head,
officials of this Office were mainly members of the Nakatomi
family, as were also the Imperial messengers sent to certain
designated shrines. The head of the Office for many
centuries (11th—19th) was a member of the Shirakawa
family, which was descended from Emperor Kazan (985—
986). When a substitute was required, this official took the
emperor's place in performing certain court rituals. The
profession of diviners was controlled for many centuries by
the Yoshida family.

At the beginning of the Restoration the hereditary priesthood was abolished and the priests were made government
officials, their appointment being the responsibility of the
government office in charge of the shrines they served.
Prior to World War II only persons of high social standing

could become the chief priests of certain important shrines. Today, the priests are private citizens and have no official status other than that which derives from their recognition by the Association of Shinto Shrines or by the shrines they serve. They hold their position by appointment of the president of the Association who acts on the recommendation of the official boards which govern their individual shrines. Of course, there are many who inherit their father's position. The priests marry and live with their families, either in quarters provided within the shrine's precincts or in ordinary private dwellings.

Being primarily a ritualist, a priest must know how to conduct the rites, ceremonies, and festivals, including the preparation and intoning of the appropriate liturgy. This training can be secured either from other priests, by attending classes sponsored by the Association of Shinto Shrines and its prefectural branches, or by enrolling in courses offered at the Kokugakuin University or some seminary. Such training qualifies a person without further examination for one of the four grades of the priesthood. Without such qualification no one is appointed as a priest by the Association of Shinto Shrines.

Each shrine is in charge of a chief priest (*gūji*), but a large shrine may have an assistant chief priest (*gon-gūji*) and several other priests of the two lower ranks (*negi* and *gon-negi*). At Ise Shrine, there is also a High Priestess (*saishu*). This is an ancient office which traditionally has been held by an Imperial princess. It was abolished in 1868, but was revived in 1946.

When not performing ceremonies or duties at the shrine, ordinary civilian clothes are worn by the priests. It is very unusual to see a shrine priest on the street in his priestly garb. Those who serve large shrines or a number of small ones—even twenty or thirty—give full time to their priestly functions. Many, however, are teachers, officials, office workers, or have some regular occupation and give only part time to shrine affairs. In such cases an assistant or a member of the family is usually on the premises to attend to the needs of worshippers and essential business. A large number of small, relatively unimportant shrines have no regular priests and receive the ministration of a priest only on festival days or by special arrangement. Some shrines have a large number of priests. At Yasukuni Shrine, for example, there are twenty-five. According to the latest available statistics of the Ministry of Education (March, 1959), there are 21,020 priests serving the 80,005 shrines.

An unusual postwar development is the emergence of women as shrine priests. This began when the wives were left in charge of shrines, while the husbands were in military service. When they did not return their widows remained in charge. Subsequently, the Association of Shinto Shrines made provisions for women to become regular priests.

The young ladies (*miko*) in white kimono and vermilion divided skirts are not, as is sometimes supposed, vestal virgins. They are the daughters of priests or local residents whose primary function is the performance of ceremonial dances before the kami; but they also engage in such minor duties as may be required. Wnen they marry their places are taken by others.

The musicians and other members of the shrine staff may or may not be priests. Most shrine priests are administrators as well as ritualists. The raising of funds and maintenance of the property is often a very heavy responsibility. In the larger shrines there are usually a number of persons who are simply employees.

Ceremonial Dress

The priest's garb is modeled after the costume of court officials of the Heian period. It has no symbolic meaning and is not intended as a means of distinguishing the clergy from laymen. When laymen perform ritual functions, if they are officials of the shrine, they also wear the garb. In accordance with ancient tradition, the color and style indicate the class or rank of the wearer.

Kimono, etc. The simplest garb consists of a kimono, a formal divided skirt, a large-sleeved outer robe which hangs to the knees, a hat, and shoes. The kimono is generally white, a color that symbolizes purity. The divided skirt may be in white or in colors which indicate the rank of the wearer, and the formal outer robe likewise may be in white or in color. In some cases, however, all the priests irrespective of rank wear only white. The informal outer robe is called in Japanese *kariginu*, that is, " hunting garment," from the fact that the style originated as a hunting garment in the Heian Period.

Hats   There are two types of headgear. The simpler form, called *eboshi*, is worn when a priest wears the low-class robe ; the more elaborate, called *kanmuri*, is worn as full ceremonial dress or high-class robe.

Eboshi

Shose   Within the shrine, the uniquely Japanese white socks (*tabi*) are worn on all ceremonial occasions. When a priest in ceremonial robes is outdoors, special black lacquered shoes made of a piece of hollowed paulownia wood, called *asa-gutsu*, are worn. The common sandals with white thongs are worn by the lower-class priests and by all priests as informal wear.

Mace   The tapering wooden slab (*shaku*), which during rituals is held at the narrow end vertically by the priests at about the level of the abdomen or is placed within the robes under the belt, is a sort of mace, that is, a symbol of the office of priest and is believed to lend dignity to his appearance.

Costumes of Girl Attendants

Like the priest's garb, the costume of the young girl attendants at shrines, including the fan which is made of cypress resembles the costume of the court dress of the Heian period. Its most noticeable features are the white kimono and the vermilion divided skirt. When performing the *kagura* the hair, which may or may not be natural, hangs down the back in a long strand and is tied with a vermilion ribbon. On the feet there are white socks (*tabi*). Outdoors ordinary sandals with white thongs are worn.

Parishes and Parishioners

Shrines not only have a close connection with their natural surroundings and local history, but they are also usually closely related to the local residents. As social conditions in ancient Japan changed, much of the mythology and records lost their meaning and authority; but the rites and ceremonies centering in the shrines acquired an enhanced significance.

In early times, while the chieftains unified their clans and conducted the communal rites, all members of the clan had both the right and obligation to participate and, according to the rules of some, to officiate at shrine functions. Thus they had a common status as clan members. Maintenance of the local shrine and participation in its rites and festivals, rather than being considered as a duty imposed from ancient times, has been considered both a right and a precious responsibility, or even an honor which was jealously guarded. The leading inhabitants of a district usually insisted, as some continue to insist even today, on their authority to carry out certain prescribed functions in connection with the shrine rites and festivals.

From an historical point of view, the centrality of blood ties is inherent in the nature of shrine worship; and where the blood relationship continues to be dominant the bond of union in a shrine is strong. But even where the blood relationship of a community is weak, there has been a common bond, irrespective of family ties, in the performance of shrine services. And this bond has continued to operate even when individuals have lived at some distance from their native communities. Wherever possible people have expected—and have been expected by their community—to return home to fulfill their obligations.

However, as distances increased and the difficulties of returning home became more formidable, branch shrines for the local and clan kami were established throughout the country, and in this way the individual was able to maintain his spiritual relationship. Yet even today it is not uncommon for many people to return to their ancestral homes to participate in the annual festivals.

The parish boundaries of shrines are often very complicated. Sometimes they overlap. Not infrequently the borders are based on ancient contours of the area which modern developments have obliterated. Moreover, as a result of the elimination of all distinction between the clan kami and the kami of the land, and the proliferation of historic shrines, not to mention the establishment of entirely new ones, many individuals today frequently find themselves related to more than one shrine either as worshippers (*sūkeisha*) or as parishioners (*ujiko*).

Shrines, such as the Grand Shrine of Ise, Meiji and Yasukuni in Tokyo, Heian in Kyoto, and the Dazaifu in Fukuoka, for example, do not have geographical areas which are regarded as parishes. In a sense all Japan is their parish and all the Japanese people are their potential worshippers.

Similarly such local shrines as those for the war-dead or local celebrities have no parish system. Nevertheless, all the local residents are regarded as worshippers, although there is no inherent tie between them and the shrines. Their attitude in such cases is essentially a matter of individual choice.

In the case of shrines dedicated to the worship of clan kami or kami having a close relationship to the land, there are definite geographical limits within which they function. Each such shrine has a parish and it is taken for granted that all local residents will assume their proper responsibility for its support. In some cases they are also expected to participate in the performance of religious functions. This is not a relationship growing out of conversion. It is because of their being Japanese, which may sound very formal and rigid to an outsider, but it has in fact a spiritual basis. The relationship between a tutelary kami and the parishioners is a spiritual relationship like that between parent and children. People are born, brought up, and live from generation to generation under the protection of the kami. Thus, the commonly accepted idea is that they all without exception have an inherent and unbreakable kami relationship.

Shrine Shinto was disestablished as a state cult in 1945, but this did not seriously affect the relationship between the shrines and the local residents. On the contrary, generally speaking, the people have continued to regard themselves as parishioners. They make small monetary gifts in connection with annual festivals, and on special occasions assist the shrines in various ways. And although when shrines were disestablished the local neighborhood associations lost their political status, these associations still continue to function in many localities as private organizations. They not only decide on neighborhood problems, but also very often constitute the controlling groups for the local shrines.

神 **III** 道

WORSHIP AND FESTIVALS

Introduction

In Shinto all life is lived in communion and in accord with the mind of the kami, which afford the devout constant protection. Daily life is regarded as "service to the kami" that is, as *matsuri*, a term generally associated with only gala occasions and elaborate processions, but which has its deeper meaning of service and worship.

Shinto rites and ceremonies commemorate life: ordinary daily life as well as the major events in the life of the individual, community, and nation. Ceremonies may be observed on such occasions in the home or in some public place, but primarily they are observed in shrines.

Shrine rites and ceremonies are intended to ward off or ameliorate any misfortune and secure or augment the cooperation of the kami in promoting the happiness and peace of the individual and the community. They include prayer for divine protection, communion with the kami, praise of the kami's virtue, comfort for the kami's mind, reports to the kami on the affairs of daily life, and pledges offering the whole life to the kami. Therefore, the ceremonies are perfomed on the assumption that a profession of faith in the kami has been made, offerings good and beautiful have been presented, the mind and body have been purified, sincerity has been fulfilled, conduct has been courteous and proper, the evil heart, selfish desire, strife, dispute, hatred and the like have been dissolved, conciliation has been practiced, and a feeling of goodwill, cooperation and affection has been realized among the people.

The ceremonies vary greatly in complexity from the simple, individual acts of worship in front of a home altar or a local sanctuary, and the morning and evening presentation of offerings by priests, to the annual festivals which in some cases include great processions with much paraphernalia and hundreds or even thousands of people participating. Generally speaking, the larger and more important shrines have more elaborate and magnificent functions, but there are some exceptions.

The Four Elements of Worship

All ceremonies, except the simple act of worship performed by an individual before a shrine, involve four elements: purification (*harai*), an offering (*shinsen*), prayer (*norito*), and a symbolic feast (*naorai*). These may be observed either simply or elaborately, depending upon the occasion. It is a distinctive feature of Shinto that kami-worship is expressed not only from the depth of one's heart, but in a concrete act of religious ritual.

Purification Purification is for the purpose of removing all pollution, unrighteousness, and evil which may hinder life according to the kami-way and the efficacy of worship. Purification may be performed by the worshippers or by priests.

Ordinarily purification is accomplished by the individual worshipper, layman, or priest, symbolically rinsing the mouth and pouring clear water over the finger tips. This is called *temizu*, literally, " hand water. " Formal purification is accomplished by a priest first reciting a prayer of purification and then waving a purification wand in the characteristic manner in front of an individual, group, or object to be purified. This is often accompanied by lightly sprinkling salt or salt water. Purification by bathing is usually called *misogi*. The ceremony of purifying the nation or the whole world is called *Ōharai*, literally, " Great Purification. "

In purifying a shrine for a festival, the buildings and paraphernalia are all cleaned and the precincts are swept. As symbols of purification, pieces of bamboo, sprigs of *sakaki*, or rice-straw rope to which paper and flax pendants are attached are hung at appropriate places.

Purification of a priest before a festival involves a period of abstinence (see page 64).

Offerings The minimum ritual requirement for the kami is a periodic presentation of offerings. Ideally this should be done daily. In some cases it is performed twice a day. If this simple act is neglected, it is believed that the kami, particularly the ancestral spirits, will be unhappy and that misfortune will be experienced often by individuals who are remiss in observing this duty. Although there are many small wayside shrines or shrines located in remote,

PLATE 8. HEIAN SHRINE, KYOTO. A panoramic view of the main buildings with the Daigokuden or Hall of State in the center.

PLATE 9. SUMIYOSHI SHRINE, OSAKA. An example of a style of shrine architecture that shows early continental influences on pure Japanese style. This shrine has three main sanctuaries for three deities.

PLATE 10. TOSHO SHRINE, NIKKO: YOMEI GATE. A magnificent example of the massive and ornate two-story type of shrine gate. The structure of this shrine is typical of the period of Shinto-Buddhism syncretism.

inaccessible areas, which appear to be neglected, there are probably very few shrines that are not cared for sometime during the year, either by a priest or some devout resident.

In shrines of any great importance, the offerings are quite elaborate and much detailed attention goes into their preparation, especially at the time of the annual festival. But whether the shrine is large or small the manner of preparing offerings is probably prescribed in considerable detail in the shrine records. Generally they are prepared in a specially designated room and purified. Then they are placed with much formality on separate dishes or trays, and carried into the sanctuary, where they are arranged on high stands, which are usually of unpainted wood. In some cases red or black lacquered stands are used that blend with the interior of the sanctuary.

The offerings generally conform to very ancient tradition; the most simple ones being rice, salt, water, and perhaps a sprig of *sakaki*. Offerings of cut flowers are also often seen, especially at wayside shrines. Considerable variety may be noted, even in the regular daily offerings, because much depends on what the individual worshippers may bring.

Four kinds of offerings are commonly presented: money, food and drink, material, and symbolic objects. Money gifts are made by tossing a coin into the offering box in front of the sanctuary or oratory, by presenting a small sum wrapped in formal paper as a gift for a special service, or by a donation in connection with receiving the shrine tablet, the reconstruction or repair of shrine property, or some other special project. Drink offerings consist mainly of water or rice wine; but sometimes other beverages may be noted. Where water is offered it may have been drawn from a sacred well in the precincts.

Food offerings may be either cooked or uncooked. Among food offerings frequently noted are : rice, fish, seaweed, vegeta-

Offerings

bles, grain, fruit and cakes. Rice offerings in many cases, especially at festival time, are in the form of dumpling-shaped cakes made of pounded rice. When the kami is regarded as an historical person, items of which the individual concerned was especially fond are also presented.

Material offerings may include a great variety of objects. From ancient times paper, silk or cotton cloth, money, jewels, weapons, and even farm implements have been common. Gifts by the Emperor, the Imperial Household, or the Association of Shinto Shrines are invariably cloth, either silk or cotton, or money may be used as a substitute. If the kami is a patron of some occupation, a characteristic product may be offered. There are instances in ancient writings of white horses, white chickens, and white boars being presented to shrines. At some shrines animal offerings are made even today. At Ise, for example, two of the Emperor's former white mounts are in special stables, and a variety of chickens, not necessarily white, may be seen wandering about the precincts. In a few cases, in place of a living horse, a life-size image of a horse may be noted standing in a stall facing a path along which worshippers pass. The one at the Fushimi Inari Shrine in Kyoto, for example, is supplied with a magnificent saddle, bridle, and other appurtenances.

Tamagushi

Symbolic offerings usually take the form of a sprig of the sacred *sakaki* tree to which are attached strips of flax and paper. The *gohei*, which stands in a central position before the inner sanctuary, is a type of symbolic offering. The various forms of entertainment, such as the dances, drama, wrestling, and archery, are in a sense also regarded as offerings to the kami.

Prayers The ceremonial prayers, that are read, or rather recited, at shrines by the priest, are in classical Japanese, which was intelligible when it was the prevailing language, but is not understood today by people unless they have made a special study of the subject. In ancient times, a great many historical and other important records were written in beautiful, rhythmic poems in order to facilitate their transmission to posterity. Prayers were also composed in this style in order that the mystic feeling embodied in the manner of addressing the kami, which had been inherited from great antiquity, might be transmitted intact to future generations. This was especially necessary because the new, short and to Japanese ears somewhat harsh Chinese words without melody, which had been introduced from the mainland and had modified the Japanese language, were not deemed suitable to preserve the meaning and spirit of the ancient ceremonies.

Until the Meiji era the prayers were composed by the priests of each shrine in any manner deemed appropriate. In April, 1875, as part of the policy to nationalize Shrine Shinto, the government took over this responsibility, prepared the prayers in accordance with the "Detailed Laws of the Engi Period," and required their use in the stated rites and festivals of all shrines. These were revised first in March, 1914, and again in 1927. Today, prayers drafted by the Association of Shinto Shrines are in general use among member shrines, but the priests are free to write their own if they wish to do so.

As a rule the prayers open with words in praise of the kami; make some reference to the origin and possibly the history of the specific rite, festival or occasion being observed; express thanksgiving, report to or petition the kami, as may be appropriate; enumerate the offerings presented; give the status and name of the officiant; and finally add some parting words of respect and awe. The prayer read at a funeral is addressed to the spirit of the deceased as a " message of condolence." It is expressed with deep emotion and is usually filled with recollections and terms of deep affection.

Sacred Feast At the end of any Shinto ceremony, except when only the simple act of worship is performed before a shrine, whether it be in a home or shrine, or for an individual, group, wedding, or grand festival, there is a sacred feast, called *naorai*, which means " to eat together with the kami." In the case of the worshippers, this consists of formally drinking a sip of rice wine served by a priest or one of the girl attendants. In the case of a shrine festival the priests, prominent laymen, and special guests gather in the priests' quarters or some other place and, after partaking solemnly of a few sips of rice wine, enjoy a relaxing and even hilarious meal at which much more wine is consumed.

Worship in the Home

Worship requires preparation. Man cannot shift his mind from the mundane to the spiritual as he transfers his body at an intersection from one street car to another. Preparation begins at home.

To awaken early, wash the face, rinse the mouth, and purify the body and mind by worshipping the kami and the ancestral spirits gives meaning to the day and enables one to begin work with a pure feeling. The kami are sincere and always guard those who have faith. One's ancestors add unseen strength and help. Thus one is able to live a righteous life.

Some homes have small private shrines in their gardens, but in most cases there is only a high shelf (*kami-dana*)

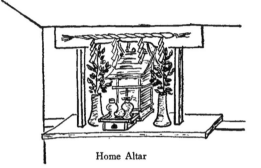

Home Altar

in some clean, quiet, convenient place on which a miniature shrine is placed. The size and quality will depend on the financial ability as well as on the faith of the head of the household. In front of the shrine there is often a small mirror, on either side of which there may be small lanterns and a sprig of *sakaki*, while above and across the length of the shelf a straw rope with small paper pendants is usually stretched. Sometimes a curtain is draped in front.

Within the shrine itself the central place is usually occupied by a talisman of the Grand Shrine of Ise placed vertically—with one for the tutelary kami on the right and one or more for any other kami that may be special objects of faith on the left. In case the shrine is small, the talisman are placed together, with the one from Ise in front, the one of the tutelary kami next, and the others behind.

For the ancestral spirits a somewhat lower, separate shelf is sometimes provided on which is placed a small box containing the memorial tablets of relatives and a mirror. Special care is taken at all times to keep the kami-shelf clean and undefiled.

The offerings, which should be fresh and presented as first fruits, consist in their simplest form of clean rice, either cooked or uncooked, water, and salt. On special occasions small portions of such things as uncooked rice, rice cakes, sea fish, wild fowl or water fowl, seaweed, vegetables, fruits, cakes or the products of the farm or garden are also offered. On ancestral

Talisman

days it is customary to offer something of which the deceased was fond, and on occasion a diploma, a certificate of appointment to a new position, the monthy salary, or similar items may be placed before the kami as a token of thanksgiving.

The procedure for worship in the home is very simple and not always uniform. Having washed the hands, rinsed the mouth, and placed fresh offerings before the kami, the worshipper stands or seats himself on a mat facing the miniature shrine and makes first a slight bow and then two deep bows. Following this whatever comes to mind as a prayer is repeated either audibly or in silence. Two deep bows, two claps with the hands in a raised position at about the level of the chest, a deep bow, a slight bow and the rite is over. Later the special food offerings are removed and served at meal time. Before eating, however, the devout Shintoist closes his eyes, slightly bows the head, and either silently or audibly claps the hand as a token of gratitude to the kami.

This, of course, is a description of the ideal behavior. In actual practice in most homes someone, probably one of the older members of the family, will tidy the shelf, change the offerings, and pause silently for a moment with hands together in an attitude of prayer. Others may or may not pay a slight token of respect as they hasten off to the work of the day.

Worship at a Shrine

On special occasions, when the local shrine is to be visited, the devout, being particularly careful in their ablutions, will put on clean linen and, after paying respect to the kami in morning devotions before the home altar and at the meal, will proceed to the shrine on foot or in some conveyance. En route, if other shrines are passed, these will be acknowledged by a bow in the direction of the sanctuary.

When the shrine compound is reached, the worshipper proceeds on foot. Passing beneath the first *torii*, a sense of being purified in heart is experienced as he walks along the path and hears the sound of crunching stone beneath his feet. No one with any illness, open wound, flowing blood, or in mourning should worship at shrines, but sometimes this taboo is not observed today. On either side of the path there may be lanterns, memorial tablets, a sacred dance pavilion, a hall for picture votive offerings, trees, and at festival time, perhaps two poles from which flags or long streamers in five colors wave in the breeze. Everything will be neat and in order because the priests will have been up for many hours already, and have swept the grounds and purified the precinct and buildings.

At the ablution pavilion the hat, scarf, and overcoat are removed. The mouth and hands are symbolically purified by the use of water taken with a wooden dipper provided for this purpose. On unusual occasions, a priest with a wooden bucket of water, dipper, and folded white paper to wipe the fingers may stand along the approach in order to provide for this rite. In front of the worship hall, after placing his hat, scarf, and overcoat to one side, the worshipper may jangle a bell, if there is one hanging over the offering box. This drives off evil spirits and produces a calm feeling by its pure sound.* Then he stands quietly and performs the simple acts of devotion by tossing a coin (in rural areas sometimes a few grains of rice wrapped in paper) into the offering box, bowing slightly first, then twice deeply, or offering a silent prayer and bowing twice deeply, clapping the hands twice at the level of the chest, bowing once deeply and then only slightly before turning away. (Sometimes a written prayer is read, but this is rather rare.)

If the occasion is one of special significance and the shrine facilities are adequate, the worshipper may make his wishes known at the shrine office and, after presenting a small

---

* Some authorities interpret the ringing of the bell as " purifying the mind," and others as " calling the attention of the enshrined kami." Ed.

money or material gift, he and those with him are taken into the oratory or sanctuary. There, sitting on the mats behind the priest who faces the inner sanctuary, a more formal ritual is observed, which includes the reading of a prayer, indicating among other things the date, occasion, names of the participants, and the presentation of a sprig of *sakaki* as a token offering. Before the ceremony begins the money or material mentioned above is placed by one of the shrine staff on the offering tables.

Simple rites of this type are requested on numerous occasions such as when a new business venture is being undertaken, when a child enters school or a youth the university, when some significant event has occurred, or to offer thanks for some special benefit.

Wedding ceremonies are also very commonly performed at shrines.

Before leaving the shrine precincts most worshippers who have come from any distance will usually stop at a stall where postcards, charms, and equipment for household shrines are available. For a small sum a number may be drawn from a box and a printed oracle received which tells what fortune or misfortune lies ahead. After a reading these oracles are usually folded and twisted around a twig of some tree or in the wire meshing of the enclosures on either side of the gates as a petition for their fulfillment, if good fortune is foretold, or for a safeguard, if the omen is unfavorable. The shrine talisman, a symbol of the kami which the worshippers can secure for a very small offering, is to be placed in a manner already described in the household altars. This consists of a piece of good quality paper on which the name of the kami is inscribed; but it may also contain a very small piece of shaving from the timbers of a former shrine building. Everything about the shrine—its buildings, its paraphernalia, its rites, its surroundings—contributes to the worship of the kami.

Festivals

Many types of shrine festivals are observed, which vary considerably in accordance with their respective traditions and local conditions. The most important occasion in any shrine is its annual or semi-annual festival (*reisai*) which is usually a spring festival (preparation for farming), an autumn harvest festival, a festival to commemorate the dedication of the shrine to the worship of one or more kami, a festival commemorating the decease of the enshrined spirit, or a festival having some significant connection with the faith of the shrine. In addition, a number of other festivals are observed which have a relationship with national traditions and seasonal customs.

Preparation of the Shrine

When an important festival approaches, shrine personnel are exceedingly busy with preparations. The buildings and compound are cleaned in advance, and on the festival day the final touches are put on the shrine compound and buildings. If not done already, small sprigs of *sakaki* are fastened on the pillars of the *torii*, fresh straw ropes with white paper pendants attached are strung in front of or below the crossbeams of the *torii* and gates, over doorways, beneath the eaves of the main buildings, and around the place for purification; and any special decorations, such as the long streamers in the five auspicious colors (white, yellow red, blue, purple), "symbolic of clouds of good omen," or trays of plants and flowers prepared by a flower arrangement society, are put in place.

Within the sanctuary, if they are not ordinarily there, brocade banners mounted on two poles capped with sprigs of *sakaki* with white paper cuttings, are often placed at either side of the offering table. To the standard on the right, silk or gold brocade bags, one containing a metal mirror and the other a string of curved stone beads (*magatama*), are attached; and to the standard on the left, a short sword, which is also enclosed in a gold brocade case, is hung. These three—the mirror, sword and jewels—although they are generally symbolic of the Imperial Regalia, are not in the shrine for that reason. They are there because it is an ancient Shinto custom to regard them as sacred.

Abstinence Preceding Festival

From the evening of the previous day those who are to officiate must prepare themselves spiritually by entering the priests' quarters, if there is one, or by secluding themselves from other people. This is called *saikai*, literally "restraint and rules" They bathe (*kessai*) frequently, put on clean clothes, take only specified food, and lead a calm and continent life, abstaining from all forbidden acts. If they violate the regulations or something occurs during this period, such as death, injury, or a fire, they are disqualified from participating in the festival and sometimes the festival itself is postponed.

The Ritual

At the designated hour the priests and musicians, some of whom may have come from other shrines to assist, the representatives of the worshippers who are to participate in the ceremony, and the bearer of the symbolic offering proceed to the purification place and, after the purification rite is performed, take their places before the inner sanctuary. Then, the assembled worshippers having been purified, the chief priest bows deeply and, as all present prostrate themselves, proceeds to open the doors of the inner sanctuary to the accompaniment of music and a weird oo-ing sound, which is said to clear the way for the kami.

The offering of food which follows is the center of the ritual. In this the various kinds of food offerings, having been ceremonially prepared and purified, are served on small wooden stands, which the priests pass from one to another until the one next in rank to the chief priest places them before the kami. During this process sacred music is played, and then a prayer is read by the chief priest.

In addition to the prescribed offerings of the shrine, there may be an offering from the Association of Shinto Shrines and, if a shrine is a very important one that is related in some way to the Royal Family, there will also be an offering from the Imperial Household. These are brought to the shrine by special messengers and separately presented by the chief priest in a somewhat more elaborate manner. Then, after each offering is made, while all present prostrate themselves, a prayer is read by the messenger. Sometimes there are sacred dances (*kagura*) by one or more of the priests, specially trained dancers, or the young maiden attendants.

Following this the chief priest and then individual worshippers, beginning with the most prominent, go forward, place on a centrally located stand a symbolic offering, that is, a sprig of the sacred *sakaki*, bow twice, clap the hands twice and then bow in an attitude of prayer before returning to their seats. In case the number of worshippers is large, one individual often acts on behalf of the majority. When this is done, all those represented stand in their places, bow, and after the sprig of *sakaki* has been laid on the stand, bow twice, clap their hands twice and bow in unison.

After this the offerings are removed by the priests and, while all prostrate themselves, the chief priest closes the doors of the inner sanctuary, again to the accompaniment of a wierd oo-ing sound. Then the priests and others who have participated directly withdraw, and finally the ceremony ends with the worshippers partaking of a symbolic feast of a sip of sacred wine, and the priests and shrine officials retiring somewhere for the concluding sacred feast (*naorai*).

In some cases, the food offerings are later shared with persons in the parish; but as a rule they are eaten by the priests and their families. When there is a quantity of rice cakes (*mochi*), they are removed after several days, and small portions are given to the parishioners.

Sacred Dances

In addition to the formal rituals at which priests officiate, most of the larger shrines make some provision, at least at their annual festivals, for the presentation of sacred dances (*kagura*) accompanied by traditional music. At many of the larger shrines dances are performed daily on request by worshippers who present a small monetary gift. The *kagura* dance, which is characteristically Japanese in its emphasis on posturing and gestures rather than the motion of the feet, is in the first instance an offering for the pleasure of the kami, and is said to have originated in the dance performed when the Sun Goddess became angry with her brother and hid in a cave. That is why performers always face the sanctuary. Nevertheless, the dances are also enjoyed and admired by the worshippers.

The *kagura*, which developed as a dance drama in the middle ages, depicts the events of the ancient Shinto mythology. There are thirty-five traditional dramas of this type. A few original dances have been created in recent years and these likewise are presented with great solemnity before the enshrined kami. *Bugaku*, the ancient court dance, came from the Asiatic continent, and has become a sort of *kagura*.

Music The musical accompaniment during the solemn part of the ceremonies and dances is patterned after the ancient court music (*gagaku*). The musicians may or may not have a priest's status.

Processions For the community-at-large, the procession is
the most exciting and at the same time the most meaningful part of a festival. The essence of the procession, as the
Japanese term meaning " august-divine-going " suggests is
the movement of the kami through the parish. This is accomplished by a symbolic transfer of the kami from the
inner sanctuary to an ornate and gilded sacred palanquin
(*mikoshi*), which becomes temporarily the abode of the kami.
Actually, the sacred symbol itself usually is not removed.
Instead, after an appropriate ritual, some symbolic substitute,
such as a sacred mirror (*shinkyo*) or a *gohei*, is used. But
in addition to the main palanquin, there are many others
made by the parishioners, including some small ones for the
children to carry. Within these, as a symbol of the kami,
is placed a piece of paper on which the kami's name is written.
Besides these palanquin it is not uncommon for a procession

Sacred Palanquin

to include beautifully decorated vehicles, somewhat resembling

PLATE 11. FUSHIMI INAHAGI SHRINE, KYOTO. Shrine rites and festivals are the highest expression of the people's faith in the kami. Above is depicted a fire festival, which is one of the special divine services.

PLATE 12. BUGAKU PERFORMANCE AT ISE. These ancient court dances are performed annually at the Grande Shrine of Ise in honor of the Imperial ancestors.

floats, on which musicians and dancers often perform.

Central in the procession, in fact, the only reason for there being a procession, is the sacred palanquin with its sacred symbol. This is generally carried on the shoulders of sturdy young men in the parish, who usually zigzag down the road jostling it up and down as they shout "wassho, wassho!" But this custom is relatively modern, and is said to be in order to make the kami happy. The ancient practice was to carry the sacred palanquin in a solemn, stately manner and this is still done by some shrines.

Usually, the sacred palanquin is carried to some place in the community where it rests for a short while, or even all night, before it is returned to the shrine. In some cases this resting place (*otabisho*) is a permanent structure, while in others a temporary shelter is erected or the front part of a home or building of a local parishioner is used. In a few instances, the resting place seems to be considered the most sacred place to the kami, the shrine itself being merely an abode for the kami between festivals. At the resting place a short ceremony, including prayer and offerings, is always observed.

As a rule, the procession may be said to have one or more of the following meanings: (1) It may signify the going out to welcome to the shrine a kami coming from a far-away world or coming down from the kami-world (*shinkai*). This may be the reason why in some cases a procession in starting from a shrine is calm, as if travelling incognito, while on the return journey it is sometimes merrily animated or proceeds in the darkness with all the lights in the shrine extinguished. (2) It may signify a visit to some place in the parish which has a special spiritual or historical significance for the kami. (3) It may be an occasion for the kami to pass through the parish and bless the homes of the faithful. (4) And finally it may commemorate the historic processions of some Imperial messengers or feudal lords on their way to the shrine.

Probably in most cases the procession has some historical significance related either to the appearance of the kami, the founding of the shrine, or some outstanding historical event in the life of the community. In a sense processions are historical religious pageants. For example, the semi-annual procession at Nikko (May and October 17) commemorates the visits of Imperial messengers to the tomb of the first shogun, Ieyasu Tokugawa; the Gion Festival (Yasaka Shrine) in Kyoto (July 17) commemorates the worship of an ancient emperor in praying for the end of a terrible plague; and the *jidai* Festival is a pageant of the manners and costumes of the period between the emperors, who had their palaces in Kyoto and who are enshrined at the Heian Shrine in that city.

Although some shrines, Meiji Shrine in Tokyo, for example, do not have sacred palanquins and hence do not hold processions, practically all of the older tutelary shrines do. However, because the significance of each procession is often unique and the different types of costumes, vehicles, and paraphernalia are so numerous, it is not possible to discuss them here in detail.

Entertainment A great many forms of entertainment are provided at a shrine or in the parish during festival time so that a festival combines both solemn and light features, and sometimes turns a whole community into something like a carnival. In practice the light features constitute entertainment for the populace, but in origin and spirit most of them in the first instance were regarded as offerings for the pleasure of the enshrined kami. This is why they are called *kan-nigiwai*, that is, " divine amusement."

Among the many forms of entertainment provided in shrines are sacred dances (*kagura*), music, classical dances (*bugaku*), archery contests, archery on horseback, (*yabusame*) horse racing, and Japanese wrestling (*sumo*).

Other forms of entertainment somewhat more hilarious, which according to their original nature are also offerings for the kami, are primarily for the enjoyment of the worshippers. Many shrines are noted for special types of entertainment which draw huge crowds from the countryside at festival time. Divine music made by drums, flutes and bells cheers the crowds. When village *kagura* plays, that is, popular *kagura*, are presented, they are usually performed by professional or local talent and include considerable humor, not to mention buffoonery, but the basis is still episodes in Shinto mythology.

神 IV 道

POLITICAL AND
SOCIAL CHARACTERISTICS

Political Life

The Meiji Restoration had two parallel and complementary objectives. One was political, the other religious. The political objective was the restoration of the direct rule of the Emperor, who for centuries had been relegated to a position of political impotence. The religious objective was to revive the Kami Way as the spiritual basis for government and society. In a sense they were identical. Consequently, it was but natural that Shinto was made the official cult of the new government.

Government Policy   The first steps toward the religious goal included an order separating Buddhism from Shinto, the establishment of a Department of Shinto modelled after the Office of Divine Affairs (Jingi Kan) of the seventh century, and a declaration to the effect that Shinto would be the religious foundation of the new government. In 1871 shrines were given official grades based on their relationship to the Imperial Family and placed under the administrative control of an appropriate national, prefectural, or local government office.

At the same time the hereditary priesthood was abolished and priests were put under the direction of the appropriate government offices in regard to appointment, support, discipline, and dismissal; but, except for the national shrines (*kankokuhei-sha*), the hereditary system continued to be generally respected. Title to all shrine property was taken over by the government in 1872 and in 1875 new rituals and ceremonies, based on the "*Detailed Laws of the Engi Period*" were promulgated for shrines of all grades. Then, on April 25, 1869, Emperor Meiji led a procession to the Ceremonial Hall of the palace, where he performed priestly functions before all the kami of the Shinto pantheon, read the Charter Oath, and explained its meaning to the assembled dignitaries. In this ceremony the new government demonstrated the re-establishment of the principle of the unity of Shinto worship and government (*saisei itchi*), which has been regarded from time immemorial as one of the fundamental concepts in the spiritual foundation of Japanese society. Thus, in every respect shrines became government institutions and Shrine Shinto became the state cult.

When exaltation of the above-mentioned Department of Shinto with the accompanying effort to suppress Buddhism failed to achieve the desired results, an Ecclesiastical Department (Kyobu Sho) was established (1872), which provided for cooperative effort on the part of both Shinto and Buddhist priests, with the latter in a position of inferiority. But this also failed and from 1874 Shinto sects were permitted to organize independently and the Buddhists were permitted to freely carry on their propaganda. In 1877 the administration of religious affairs was transferred to a Bureau of Shrines and Temples in a newly organized Ministry of Home

Affairs, and in 1882 a distinct line was drawn between shrine priests and other religious teachers. Moreover, a distinction was made between shrines as national, non-religious community-morality establishments and the temples and churches. Then, in 1900 this bureau was divided into a Bureau of Shrines and a Bureau of Religions, and thirteen years later the Bureau of Religions was transferred to the Ministry of Education. In this way, the administration of shrines was separated from the general field of religion and it seemed that a relatively permanent arrangement had been devised for dealing with both Shrine Shinto and religion.

Many Shintoists, however, were far from satisfied and with the development of the so-called "Showa Restoration Movement" in the nineteen-thirties a demand again arose, as in the Meiji Restoration, for the re-establishment of an Office of Divine Affairs (Jingi Kan) as a department of government having precedence over the regular cabinet ministries. Yet, in spite of the great pressure exerted at that time, all that could be achieved was the creation of a Divine Affairs Board (Jingi-in) within the Ministry of Home Affairs.

Defeat, surrender, and a military occupation brought about a revolutionary change in the status of Shrine Shinto. As a result of the Shinto Directive, shrines were disestablished as state institutions and the observance, support, and sponsorship of Shinto rites and teachings in any form by any government agency were strictly forbidden. Finally, the Constitution incorporated in its provisions the basic principles of religious freedom, and a rigid separation of religion and state became the law of the land. Today,

Shinto shrines have no relation with the state. They are private institutions supported and managed entirely by the shrine parishioners and worshippers.

The State The Shinto faith brings not only the individual, the neighborhood and society into direct relationship with the kami and makes them more ideal; it does the same for the political world. Even in ancient times when Japan had not yet become well unified, the clans regarded shrine rites as an important factor in political life, and as the country become consolidated this attitude became more pronounced. The intimate manner in which, throughout the centuries, Shinto has been connected with the political state is evident in many ways. On the one hand, the court rites already mentioned have been observed exclusively by the Imperial Family, that is, the state; while on the other hand, the performance of shrine worship has been primarily a function of the people, and the state has made offerings at the shrines for the peace and welfare of the country.

According to the mythology, when the Imperial ancestor, Ninigi-no-mikoto, descended from heaven and secured the allegiance of Okuni-nushi, the Kami of Izumo, he promised in return to build a sacred palace, that is, a shrine, and serve the kami eternally. This is the origin of the Grand Shrine of Izumo, which is located on the west coast of Japan in Shimane Prefecture near the city of Matsue.

Moreover, from earliest times the emperors, regarding the Sun Goddess as their ancestress in faith, have employed hereditary ritual officials to perform kami-rites for the court. Some of these are purely ancestral rites for the Imperial Family. Others are political in nature. The distinction is not always clear. Some, such as the Great Purification, for example, concern the entire country. Others, such as the wedding of the Crown Prince, concern primarily the Imperial Family.

In ancient society, the emperor and high court officials, in a sense were mainly ritualists who carefully observed certain rites and practices for the purpose of insuring the happiness of the people and the peace of the country. Government meant the guidance of society in the cooperative performance of kami-rites, which it was believed would produce communal tranquility. Worship, that is, the performance of these kami-rites, was a fundamental element in government itself. The word *matsurigoto*, literally, "worship affairs," covered what would be regarded today as both religious rites and civil administration, but was formerly considered to be a single, undifferentiated experience. This was true on a local as well as a national level. The festivals and rites for the various tutelary kami and the administration of clans and local society were essentially a single function. A term that describes this identity of kami-rites and civil administration is *saisei itchi*, which means the unity (*itchi*) of worship (*sai*) and government (*sei*).

Throughout history the palace rites have been prescribed by law. In a legal code promulgated in the Taiho era*

---

* The code that we have now is not the Taiho Code itself, but the code as amended in 718 in the Yoro era.

(670—720) there were twenty articles related to Shinto which dealt mainly with court rites. The *Detailed Laws of the Engi Period* prescribed the ceremonies for shrines related to the Imperial Family, the offering of prayers (*norito*) at shrines, and a list of kami (3,132) venerated by the state.

After the Shogunate was established the care of Shinto establishments was neglected, but early in the Meiji Restoration most of them were revived.

Just as the *Kojiki, Nihon Shoki,* and the other writings already mentioned, were vehicles for the transmission of the dynastic claims of the Imperial Family and the clans, so the shrines, which constituted the ritual basis for maintaining the unity of the local community established on the dual foundation of a common clan and a common geographical relationship, became national institutions and were expected to conduct rites for the kami in the name of the state. At the same time the state along with the people offered thanks to the kami and prayed not only for the peace of the country and the welfare and prosperity of the land, but also that those in positions of political responsibility would, with sincere faith, perform their duties in a spirit of fairness and service. This change of focus from the immediate locality to the entire nation reflected the political change which was effected when loyalty to the clan ruler was superseded by loyalty to the national ruler, and the shrines welcomed the change as being consonant with their essential character.

Broadening the shrine's horizon had the salutary effect of enlarging the outlook of the worshippers, and from this standpoint nationalization was beneficial for both the shrines and the people. Thus, it was the ideal of State Shinto to become the political conscience of the country.

However, with the disestablishment of Shinto in 1945 the rites of the court, on the one hand, including the sending of Imperial messengers to certain shrines, became the responsibility of the Imperial Family and constitute what is known today as Imperial Household Shinto, while the shrines became private religious institutions controlled by their respective priests and representatives of the parishioners.

In a great many cases the shrines are very flourishing. The reason for this is relatively simple. The effect of the abolition of State Shinto and the disestablishment of shrines was not as serious as some feared because, while from ancient times shrines have had a very close relationship with the state, the sponsoring of shrine rites has always been the responsibility of the people themselves.

Nationalism   Shinto has been generally regarded abroad as synonymous with ultranationalism, militarism, and emperor worship.   This is not strange because Shinto was unquestionably used by the militarists and those in power to unify the mind and strengthen the loyalty of the people. It was probably inevitable historically that this should have happened.   Threatened with oppression and even absorption by Buddhism and Confucianism, Shinto became a bulwark for the preservation and independence of the racial culture.

From the beginning of the seventeenth century the fear of intrusion from Western nations resulted in the suppression of Christianity and the exclusion of foreigners.   In the first half of the nineteeth century the expanding power of an imperialistic Occident jeopardized the country's long history of independence. Threatened thus by invasion from without and suffering from serious evils caused by feudalism within, many leaders longed for a revival of the days when the emperor himself would again rule the land. In this situation it was only natural that Shinto, which had a close relationship with the Imperial Family and had experienced oppression and even absorption by Buddhism and Confucianism, should become the spiritual basis for the preservation and independence of the racial culture, and the protection of the country from alien domination.

Consequently Shinto acquired a very nationalistic character and it was natural that during World War II patriotism would find in it a source of strong spiritual support. Indeed, Shinto then seemed to have an exclusively nationalistic character. However, fundamentally, Shinto is a faith which is based on the belief that the many kami cooperate together. Shrine Shinto is worship to unite and harmonize the various kinds of kami. The spirit of tolerance and cooperation is a hitherto unnoticed aspect of Shinto. Since the war's end, as a result of reflection upon the narrow-minded nationalism of the past, this unnoticed aspect is coming to be increasingly recognized.

Emperor Worship Central in the movement to develop a modern state was the enhancement of veneration for the Emperor as the foundation of the state ; and in this shrines played a most important role. Yet it is an interesting fact that only relatively few shrines are dedicated to the worship of specific emperors. Including Emperor Ojin, who is worshipped at Hachiman shrines, which constitute a special case and number many thousands, only twenty of the 124 rulers of Japan have special shrines in their honor.

Among these twenty emperors, seven met with misfortune and their enshrinement takes the form of consolation of their spirits for the mistreatment accorded them. In addition, eleven Imperial princes are enshrined, all of whom sacrified their lives in loyal and valiant service to the throne. The most famous shrines to emperors are Kashiwara Shrine in Nara Prefecture and Miyazaki Shrine in Kyūshū, where the Emperor Jimmu is venerated; Heian Shrine in Kyoto, which is dedicated to the Emperor Kammu, who founded the capital in Kyoto, and Emperor Komei, the last one to reside in Kyoto before the capital was moved to Tokyo; and Meiji Shrine, where the spirits of Emperor Meiji and his consort, Empress Shoken, are enshrined.

In spite of nationalization and the extreme perversion of the shrines and emperor worship by the militarists and ultranationalists, it does not seem that the emphasis on emperor worship and the accompanying pressures in connection with shrine worship in the past century necessarily brought the people under the special influence of those particular shrines that had a close relationship with the Imperial Family and the foundation of the nation. Today, some of the important shrines, which hold a unique position in the mythology of the nation, are in serious financial straits, while other equally important ones, are flourishing in spite of the loss of state support. In the case of the Grand Shrine of Ise, for example, which has the closest connection of any with the Imperial Family, it may be noted that the shrine saw its greatest prosperity in the pre-Meiji Era at the time when the influence of the Imperial court was at low ebb. Thus, it can be seen that the faith of the populace itself and not government pressure really determines the popularity of shrines.

Hakko Ichi-u When anyone looks closely at the shrines and understands the rites, which are performed as the people pray for peace and prosperity amidst the beauty of the countryside and the joyous atmosphere of the festivals, he can clearly understand how far removed the spirit of shrine worship is from reckless acts of violence. Among the expressions most frequently thought to typify world military expansion, none has been quoted more frequently than "*Hakko Ichi-u*," which means "To cover the eight corners of the world under one roof." Yet when originally used by the first emperor it meant to bring peace and establish an ideal state.

The harmony and reconciliation which are the essence of Shrine Shinto, are nowhere better expressed than in a poem by the Emperor Meiji, who wrote,

> "When all the seas, I deem, are our brethren,
>
> 四方の海　みなはらからと思ふ世に
>
> Why do the winds and waves noisily rise?"
>
> など波風の　立ちさはぐらん

The Association of Shinto Shrines (Jinja Honcho) expresses the true feelings of the people and the true nature of Shrine Shinto in the following three foundation principles:

1. To express gratitude for divine favor and the benefits of ancestors, and with a bright, pure, sincere mind to devote ourselves to the shrine rites and festivals.
2. To serve society and others and, in the realization of ourselves as divine messengers, to endeavor to improve and consolidate the world.
3. To identify our minds with the Emperor's mind and, in loving and being friendly with one another, to pray for the country's prosperity and for peaceful co-existence and co-prosperity for the people of the world.

Thus, the shrines today as in the past endeavor to fulfill their mission to become the political conscience of the people.

THE ARTS

Shrines as a rule do not have images as objects of worship.* Generally speaking, only symbolic objects are used for this purpose, and these are kept within the holy of holies. No one is ever allowed to see them.** Consequently, in comparison with Buddhism and Hinduism, for example, there has been relatively little Shinto art. Nevertheless, Shinto has made a not inconsiderable contribution to the

---

* This statement will surprise many who have heard that there are no images in shrines. As a matter of fact there are very few. The oldest of such images (jinzo) are two at the Matsuo Shrine on the outskirts of Kyoto.
** An exception to this prohibition occurred early in the Meiji Restoration when government officials inspected the shrines and temples to determine whether the structures should be classified as shrines or temples.

field of art indirectly through the use of images of guardian animals, the employment of the finest artists and artisans in the construction and decoration of sanctuaries, in the making of gardens, and in the preservation of natural beauty surrounding shrines. Moreover, by encouraging the presentation of the finest products of one's skill as offerings to the kami, it has provided an incentive for those with special skills to exert themselves to the utmost to achieve perfection of expression, and some shrines have been responsible for more than a thousand years for the preservation and transmission of ancient techniques.

Although there is no great amount of distinctly Shinto literature, the kami-faith has furnished countless subjects for poets, many of whom have presented their masterpieces to the kami as offerings. The same is the case with calligraphers, painters, and sculptors. Furthermore, through the preservation of the sacred dances (*kagura*) and patronage of classical music (*gagaku*) and dances (*bugaku*), drama (*Noh*), and the transmission of popular forms of local entertainment, such as village drama (*sato kagura*), the shrines have made a lasting contribution to these fields of art.

The most unique contribution, however, has been in the field of shrine architecture, which is best epitomized in the Grand Shrine of Ise. Bruno Taut, the famous critic, in his *Houses and People of Japan* says that

> The shrines of Ise are Japan's greatest and completely original creation in general world architecture. We encounter here something entirely different from the most beautiful cathedrals, mosques, the Indian and Siamese temples or pagodas, and even from the temples of China. The Parthenon on the Acropolis is to the present day a visible sign of the

beautiful gifts that the men of Athens bestowed on their symbol of wisdom and intelligence, Athena. It is the greatest and most aesthetically sublime building in stone as are the Ise shrines in wood.

Economic Life

Shinto is concerned not only with the sacred but also with the secular. Commercial and industrial activities, everything necessary for the production of food, clothing and shelter, everything for the development of culture and giving happiness to the world, has a direct connection with the kami. Commercial activities which are closely connected with the kami are good. Those that promote one's own happiness, should also promote the happiness of society. But this is not enough. We are happiest when we make others happy. If commercial life is not directly connected with the kami, it is bad and drives us toward misfortune.

Shinto does not look lightly upon material things. It does not regard the absence of material goods as admirable, nor does it regard the desire for things as necessarily evil. On the contrary, it considers such a desire as a natural development of a life of adoration of the kami. Consequently, as long as the desire for material things is related to the kami, and is for the sake of the public welfare, it is good and must be blessed by the kami. But seeking after and using wealth for selfish purposes or in ways that injure others is not in accord with the way of the kami.

When Japan was primarily an agricultural country, through the shrine festivals the people sought after good crops in the spring and expressed gratitude for rich harvest in the fall. Throughout the season prayers were offered for pro-

PLATE 13. TOGAKUSHI JINJA, NAGANO. A performance of the *mikomai*, one of the main types of female Shinto dance. The young girls in the picture each carry a small baton with bells.

PLATE 14. YOSHIDA JINJA, KYOTO. Girl dancers with their flowery headdresses perform divine service at the annual spring festival.

PLATE 15. MINATOGAWA JINJA, HYOGO. The kami or a symbolic substitute travels through the streets on festival days, born aloft in an ornate and gilded "divine palanquin."

tection against destructive wind, rain, drought, and insects. In spirit this took the form of making an offering of the first fruits to the kami, and in expressing thanks for the "remnant" left for personal use. This practice continues today in rural areas, and the same is true for those engaged in hunting, fishing, industrial arts, industry and commerce. All offer prayers of petition and thanksgiving.

The holding of fairs and markets in the precincts of shrines developed from the custom of people coming together at festival time to make offerings to the kami and then exchanging goods (divine gifts). The word meaning market (*ichiba*), implies a "sacred place." Medieval commerce and industry developed under the shadow of large Buddhist temples and Shinto Shrines. This was not especially related to Shinto, but arose from the government policy of protecting religion. Nevertheless, it accorded with the basic spirit of the relationship between shrines and the economic life of the parishioners. The shrine festival itself involves great expense and draws many visitors. Markets are set up, which contribute much to the communities, but they also may sometimes cause difficulty by the misuse of the festival.

Historical Relations with Other Religions

When Confucianism and Buddhism were introduced into Japan from the Chinese mainland during the fifth and sixth centuries, some conflict took place between Shinto and Buddhism. Later, in the eighth century, a compromise was reached which resulted in the teaching that the kami were pleased to receive Buddhist sutras as offerings and to hear them recited in worship. As a consequence Buddhist temples were established alongside shrines, ostensibly to satisfy the kami, make them into Buddhist believers, and finally raise them to the level of buddhas. (At the beginning of the nineteenth century there were many such temples adjacent to even small shrines.) Then in the ninth century some shrine kami became the guardians of Buddhist temples. For example, the kami of Hiyoshi Shrine in Sakamoto at the foot of Mount Hiei became the guardian of the Tendai monastery, Enryakuji, and the kami of Nibutsu Hime Shrine in Wakayama Prefecture was the protector of the Shingon monastery, Kongobuji, on Mount Koya.

Moreover, a syncretistic faith taught by Buddhists emerged which claimed that the buddhas were the prime noumenon, while the kami were their Japanese manifestations. In Shingon Buddhism for example, the Sun Goddess was said to be the avatar of the Cosmic Buddha.

Thus in later centuries each major division of Buddhism developed its own special variety of syncretism to correspond to its sectarian doctrine. In the 13th century Tendai Buddhism developed Sanno Shinto, and Shingon Buddhism Ryōbu (Dual Aspect) Shinto,* and in the 15th century, Nichiren Buddhism propounded Hokke Shinto.

One illustration of how this trend manifested itself may

---

* The term " *ryōbu* " has two usages. In the first instance it was applied in Shingon Buddhism to two aspects of the universe, the noumenal and the phenomenal. Later it was combined with the word "Shinto" to describe the concept that Shinto kami were Japanese manifestations of Buddhist deities (*honji suijaku*).

be seen in the erection in the 17th century of the three famous Hachiman Shrines (Usa Hachiman-gu, Iwashimizu Hachiman-gu, and Tsurugaoka Hachiman-gu,) and the To-shogu at Nikko, the latter being based on Sanno Ichijitsu Shinto, a branch of Sanno Shinto.

However, Shinto leaders could not view with equanimity this attempt of a foreign religion to absorb the indigenous faith, so at the same time in the 13th and 14th centuries a reaction set in, which produced several counter-movements aimed at placing Shinto in a position of ascendancy. One such was Yui-itsu or Yoshida Shinto, which first appeared in the early 13th century, but was not fully developed until the 15th century when Kanetomo Yoshida became its proponent and made his slogan: " Kami, primary, Buddha secondary." Another was Ise Shinto, also known as Watarai Shinto. Although tolerant toward Buddhism, Ise Shinto stressed purity and sincerity as the highest virtues, faithfully maintained the purity of its tradition, and firmly rejected the idea that Buddhist deities were the manifestation of the prime noumenon. These two schools, along with several others, were the forerunners of Revival Shinto of which Norinaga Motoori (1730—1801) and Atsutane Hirata (1776 —1843), who claimed to advocate " pure " Shinto, were the outstanding exponents.

It was Revival Shinto that became dominant and finally provided important spiritual motivation for the Meiji Restoration of 1868. But the effort to revive " pure " Shinto was only partially successful. To be sure, most of the Buddhist elements were eliminated from Shinto shrines, but it was impossible to remove them all. In the thousand years of syncretism the relationship had become too close. The effect of Buddhism on Shinto architecture was, of course, ineradicable, but there were other cases also, such as Inari worship in the Toyokawa Inari, for example, where the separation movement failed.

Modern Relations with Other Religions

Historically on a local level there has always been cooperation between shrines and other religious institutions. Cooperation on a "denominational" or national level is a postwar phenomenon. Today the Association of Shinto Shrines is active as one of the five associations which constitute the Religions League of Japan (*Nihon Shūkyō Renmei*), the other four being the Japan Buddhist Federation (*Zen Nippon Bukkyō Kai*), the Sectarian Shinto Federation (*Nihon Kyōha Shinto Renmei*), the Christian Liaison Committee (*Kirisutokyō Rengo Kai*), and the Union of New Religious Organizations of Japan (*Shin Nippon Shūkyo Dantai Rengo Kai*). Moreover, it encourages local shrines to cooperate in the Japan Council for Interfaith Cooperation (*Nihon Shūkyō Kyōryoku Kyōgi Kai*).

This interest in associating with other religious organizations may seem somewhat strange but, since its fundamental spirit is one that emphasizes harmony and cooperation, it is only natural that Shrine Shinto should be tolerant and friendly toward other religious bodies and approve of the parishioners affiliating with them. Under government control shrine worship was regarded as transcending rather than conflicting with the acceptance of another religious faith, and this seems to be an ideal which does not limit the religious faith of shrine worshippers. But until government control was withdrawn it was not possible for the shrine world to cooperate. Today, however, the inherent tendency of Shrine Shinto has come to the surface and the Association of Shinto Shrines is actively participating in the religious world on all levels.

Dual Faith As far as Shrine Shinto is concerned the so-called dual religious affiliation of the parishioners is taken as a matter of course. Not only is there no objection on the part of shrines to their parishioners being adherents of some denomination of Buddhism, Christianity, Shinto, or some other religion ; it is assumed that they will. Shrine Shinto regards the shrines as something distinctly different from the institutions of other religions and in no way in conflict with them. But Shrine Shinto leaders, while being deeply interested in the activities of the religious world and eager to promote common causes, are concerned about the unfavorable restrictions which they must accept because of being classified with other religions. Therefore, the Association of Shinto Shrines is seeking ways to remove these handicaps.

Everyday Customs

As in most countries there is a close relationship in Japan between many common customs and the indigenous faith of the people. Shrine worship consists primarily in the celebration of the events of daily life, great and small, personal and communal, so it is natural that many of the common customs of the people should be closely associated with, if not actually derived from, Shrine Shinto practices.

At New Year's time the people decorate their homes with the traditional symbols of Shinto and as early as possible on New Year's Day worship their tutelary kami, famous shrines, and shrines located in fixed directions. Originally, New Year's Day fell at the close of winter and ushered in the spring. Then came the festival of rice planting, prayers for good crops, thanksgiving for the harvest and the Great Purification in the middle and at the end of the year. Some of these have been taken over by Buddhists, but historically they are in fact derived from primitive Shinto customs.

While probably of Chinese rather than indigenous origin, the Girl's Festival of March 3, the Boy's Festival of May 5, and the Star Festival of July 7 are popularly regarded as closely related to Shinto.

After the land has been cleared and before construction of a building is begun, a ceremony of purifying the site and consoling the land kami is always observed. Formerly this was done by the people concerned without outside assistance, but now it is customary to call in a shrine priest to officiate. Completion of the frame of a new building is celebrated by placing a symbol of the presence of the kami (*gohei*) at the center of the ridge pole and the passing out of rice cakes, sweets, and rice wine to the workers and neighbors. This is known as the the " Ceremony of Placing the Ridge Pole" (*jōtō-sai*), although generally no priest is present.

The semi-annual house-cleaning, which in modern times is observed throughout the nation in spring and fall as a sanitary measure promoted by local public health officials, is a development of the Great Purification ceremony of ancient Shinto, although the original meaning has been almost completely forgotten by the general public. The custom of settling accounts in June and December is of the same derivation. Moreover, in the business world there is a custom of merchants clapping their hands when a business deal has been successfully negotiated or when a dispute has been amicably settled, thus calling the kami to witness the consummation of the matter.

It can be seen from these illustrations, which are only a few of the many that might have been used, that there is a very close relationship between Shinto customs and the everyday life of the people.

神 **V** 道

SOME SPIRITUAL CHARACTERISTICS

Transmission of the Faith

S hrine Shinto has always been so intimately associated with the daily life of the people that little need has been felt to formulate Shinto thought into any doctrinal system. The kami faith itself, participation in its rites, and the observance of Shinto-related customs have been taken as a matter of course by the individual and community. In the transmission of Shinto from generation to generation not much attention has been given to the philosophical or doctrinal expositions of the faith. Efforts have been made to preserve the record of shrine history and customs, but very little literature has been written to aid worshippers in understanding the nature of the enshrined kami and the meaning of shrine rites and practices.

How then has the faith been transmitted from generation to generation, from century to century, through more than two milleniums? It has been caught and not taught. Dependence has been placed almost entirely on the sensory appeal of the rites and festivals, as well as of the shrines themselves. The kami-faith was transmitted from heart to heart through daily life.

It is not easy to express the meaning of this faith in

creed, doctrine, or philosophy. Yet, even though a systematic exposition may be lacking, there can be no question but that after the spiritual wandering and indifference of youth have spent their course, the sensory appeal, the feeling of awe and mystery, and the consciousness of a relationship with the past which these engender bring many an individual back to the patrimonial shrine and the only spiritual home he has ever known. The strength of Shrine Shinto is in its emphasis on sensory experience derived from mystic rites and natural phenomena rather than on theological discourses. Thus, the kami-faith is one that is maintained through the observance of traditional ways rather than by overt propaganda.

Except for the pre-war teaching in public schools in connection with history and morals, Shrine Shinto has never had anything that resembles religious education. During the eighty years of government supervision, any such activity on the part of shrines themselves was forbidden. Consequently, it is not strange that many people, even some who are professionally associated with shrines, are unable to state in clear, succinct language the nature of Shinto. This does not mean, however, that the layman, who says he knows nothing about Shinto, has disassociated himself from the shrines or has lost interest in shrine practices. Many parishioners are hardly aware of the extent to which they are linked to and unconsciously controlled by the shrine and all that it means.

There is a tingle of excitment, a thrill of joy as one enters into a grove which surrounds a shrine, or stands within view of the *torii* and sanctuary as a ritual is being performed. Especially at the Grand Shrine of Ise, the magnificent cryptomeria and cypress trees create within the devout an inexpressible feeling of awe and wonder. When young men in *happi* coats and with towels wrapped tightly about their heads shout *"wassho, wassho,"* as they zigzag down the streets with the sacred palanquin hoisted on their shoulders, they experience an exhilaration unimagined by those who do not enter into the spirit of the occasion. The kami-faith is caught not taught; and the experience begins when a baby is first carried to the shrine on the mother's back.

This method of transmission from life to life and heart to heart throughout the ages might have been insufficient if Shinto had been a matter of individual faith centering in the acceptance of certain doctrines or a creed. But historically Shinto has involved the observance of communal rituals in which both leaders of the national and local governments publicly officiated and all the people participated. Naturally, then, it is difficult for outsiders to understand Shrine Shinto, even though every effort is made to explain it. In some cases, such as Lafcadio Hearn, for example, it is possible to understand the Shinto way of thinking without really understanding Shinto.

Prayer-Priests The nearest the shrines ever came to engaging in propaganda was in the Middle Ages when the system of prayer-priests (*oshi*) came into existence. These were not regular priests. They lived in separate buildings close to certain large shrines, some of which were far from the centers of population. There they provided lodging accommodations for pilgrims, distributed shrine charms, offered prayers, and led the pilgrims to the shrine sanctuaries where obeisance was offered to the kami. Thus, they were very useful in developing the faith of the pilgrims. However, when the Meiji government forcibly separated the shrines from Buddhism, and ordered the separation of the shrine priests from the teachers of " Sectarian Shinto," this prayer-priest system was officially abolished. As a result, although the system has survived in a modified form in some instances and can be observed even today, the influence of shrines in isolated regions has greatly declined.

Associations Associations (*kōsha*) of worshippers constituted a second type of propaganda agency. These developed throughout the country in more recent times in order to promote the worship of certain kami and in some cases the observance of certain somewhat unique religious practices. In addition to this they also served as cooperatives for raising funds so that annually one or more of their number could go on a pilgrimage. Some associations were developed by prayer-priests (*oshi*), but sometimes they were informal, local organizations of worshippers, and were not in any way directly connected with any shrine. When the Meiji government nationalized the shrines some of these associations, notably those that worshipped the Grand Shrine of Izumo, Mount Fuji, and Mount Ontake, became sects of what is known as " Sectarian Shinto." Others, such as those centering in the worship of Ise and Fushimi Inari continued to exist without following their example. In recent years, as travel has become easier and excursion buses more common, these associations have diminished in importance. In their heyday, however, they were very effective propaganda agencies.

Primarily, shrines have depended on the development of a close relationship with the parishioners to foster the kami-faith. To accomplish this, participation in the activities related to shrine festivals has been considered most effective. However, at the end of World War II, when the supervision of the shrines by the government was abolished, the relationship tended to deteriorate and the shrines needed to devise some means of training new worshippers. Hence, regardless of what the conditions were in the past, the necessity for some propaganda activities has become very evident. To meet this situation some literature has been produced for both the priests and people, and lectures and audio-visual techniques have been promoted both nationally and locally.

Moreover, while shrines have always been centers of considerable community activity, which helped to maintain the interest of the local residents, in recent years this phase of shrine life has greatly increased. For example, besides directly sponsoring meetings in the shrines for children, youth and adults, especially classes in flower arrangement and meetings for local community organizations, a number of shrines have added new structures or have used their facilities for kindergartens, nursery schools, and playgrounds. That there are now (1961) 180 organized shrine kindergartens may not seem significant to the outsider but, when it is remembered that no activities of this nature were permitted when the shrines were national institutions, this development is impressive. Thus, today in addition to the traditional activities related to the festivals, shrines are contributing to social welfare, and in this way, rather than by the spread of doctrine, faith in the kami is being strengthened. This is not to say that more must not be done in the development of teachings, but the shrines will probably never depend as much on preaching and teaching as do other religions.

Shrines and Nature

Irrespective of the enshrined kami, the shrines themselves cannot be considered without some reference to their relation to the natural beauty which traditionally has surrounded them. Shrine worship is closely associated with a keen sense of the beautiful,—a mystic sense of nature which plays an important part in leading the mind of man from the mundane to the higher and deeper world of the divine and in transforming his life into an experience of living with the kami. No amount of artificial beauty is an adequate substitute for the beauty of nature. Throughout the country the most beautiful spot in any community is generally the site of a shrine.

City life, of course, tends to crowd out much, if not all, of the natural beauty that has been considered an essential element for shrines. This cannot be helped, and downtown city shrines have adapted themselves to the inevitable lack of much natural beauty in their surroundings; but this does not alter the fundamental fact that ideally shrines should be located where the mind of man can be brought close to nature. Hence, in order to adequately understand shrine worship, it is necessary to consider those located in the midst of groves or forests, unaffected by the modern city.

Most noteworthy of all such shrines are the Toshogu at Nikko and the shrines at Ise. At Nikko the structures are elaborate and ornate, and are located on a mountain side. At Ise they are plain and undecorated, and are situated on relatively level ground. Yet the beauty of the buildings in both cases harmonizes completely with the world of nature, especially the magnificent cryptomeria which tower above. Visitors, whether devout or profane, can hardly leave without being deeply impressed.

Tree Worship Tree worship is very common in Shinto. Whether a shrine stands silently in the midst of a small grove by the wayside or within the limits of a bustling city, town, or village, the worshipper will find the presence of trees a help in his approach to the kami. A great many shrines, perhaps the majority, are still located within small groves and some are in forests. In rural areas especially, the devout are reminded of the nearness of the kami simply by looking towards the wooded area in which a shrine is nestled. This close relationship between trees and shrines can be seen in the ancient use of the word meaning "forest" (*mori*) to designate a shrine, and the word meaning "shelter of a kami" (*kannabi*) for the surrounding woods.

Within the precincts there is frequently one tree in particular which is regarded as especially sacred and is protected by an enclosure or has a straw rope around its trunk from which short paper strips depend. These trees are believed to be the special abode of some kami. In primitive times people believed that through such trees the spirit of the kami could be understood; but today the tree is only an expression of the divine consciousness.

A different kind of sacred tree is one that has a peculiar shape and is thought to possess unique qualities derived from the kami or the divine spirit which uses the tree as its abode. Such trees may or may not be within the precinct of a shrine. Quite often there are small *torii* and other Shinto symbols at their base. In a few rare cases, there are shrines with only an oratory which regard a single tree, a grove or a forest as the object of worship. One such shrine is Ten'itsu Jinja in Sakurai City, Nara Prefecture. But perhaps one of the most significant indications of this general regard for trees is the fact that the *sakaki* is a sacred tree of Shinto and is always used in formal rituals.

Sacred Mountains Lofty mountains, like groves and forests, also play an important role in creating an atmosphere of dignity for shrines. In not a few cases shrines are located on lonely summits or on the slopes of mountains far removed from any community,—a fact which vividly illustrates the point that shrines are not places for propaganda or evangelism, but are primarily sacred dwelling places for kami.

Mountain worship is one of the oldest types of Shinto. In ancient times many of Japan's famous mountains were regarded as sacred, but today most of them are no longer special objects of worship.

A mountain, which is regarded as the dwelling of a kami is called a "spirit mountain" (*reizan*) or a "divine body mountain" (*shintai-zan*). In very ancient times there were, of course, no shrine buildings for this type of worship. None were deemed necessary. But in the course of the centuries pavilions, that is, worship halls, were erected and subsequently many sanctuaries were also constructed with a symbolic object in the holy of holies as a "divine body."

In a few cases, where the mountain has remained visible, no sanctuary has been erected. Only an oratory exists to provide facilities for worship. One such is the Ōmiwa Shrine in Nara Prefecture which, except for the absence of a main sanctuary, has other characteristic buildings. Opposite the entrance of the oratory and facing the sacred mountain is an opening in which a split bamboo curtain is hung and before which are placed the usual paraphernalia of worship, including tables for offerings. Because the mountain itself is regarded as sacred, none except the priests are ever allowed to ascend it or even to enter the area. Nowadays usually the mountain is not worshipped as the kami, but is regarded as a sacred place appropriate for worshipping the kami or for meditating on spiritual matters.

The most famous sacred mountain in Japan is, of course, Mount Fuji, which is devoted to the worship of Kono-hana-sakuyahime-no-mikoto, consort of Ninigi-no-mikoto, great grandfather of the first emperor. On the edge of the crater is a small shrine, while at several places around the base of the mountain are large shrines dedicated to this same kami. The principal one of these is at Fujinomiya in Shizuoka Prefecture.

Mount Nantai near Nikko is another famous sacred mountain. In this case the main shrine, Futarasan Shrine, is in Nikkō near the Toshogū, the Inner Shrine is at the peak, and an intermediate shrine is located near the shore of Lake Chūzenji. The annual festival in August features an ascent of the mountain participated in by tens of thousands of worshippers, most of whom start from the intermediate shrine by the lake.

The phenomenon of mountain worship in Japan is not limited to Shinto. There are sacred mountains in Buddhism also, and there is a special type of Shinto-Buddhistic faith, called Shugen-do, which is famous for its priests, who are called *yamabushi* (mountain ascetics), but a discussion of these is outside the scope of this volume.

Other Natural Objects : Caves, Rocks, etc.

Other natural objects, such as rock and caves, are also venerated as the abode of the kami. For example, a cave on the island of Enoshima near Kamakura is sacred to the Enoshima Shrine, which worships the kami Benten. The largest and most famous sacred cave in Japan is in Miyazaki Prefecture where the sanctuary of the Udo Shrine stands within the cave itself. The object of worship there is the spirit of the father of Jimmu Tenno, Japan's first emperor who is said to have been born in this cave. Suwa Shrine in Nagano Prefecture has a rock as its object of worship; the Itsukushima Shrine in Hiroshima Prefecture worships the island, Miyajima, on which it stands; and the Kumano Shrine in Wakayama Prefecture is dedicated to the worship of the Nachi waterfalls.

The World, Man, Salvation, and Death

The World In ancient Shinto, the idea of another world was expressed by such concepts as the High Plain of Heaven (Takama-ga-hara), the dwelling place of the most august kami, the Country of Abundant, Eternal Life (Tokoyo-no-kuni), and the world of dead ghosts, evil spirits (*magatsuhi*) and pollution, that is, the World of Darkness (Yomi-no-kuni). Modern Shrine Shinto, however, does not present such traditional explanations to the people. There is considerable uncertainly regarding them. Moreover, such metaphysical concepts are not directly related to the people, and to look upon the spirits of the other world is regarded as taboo. Instead of developing theoretical explanations of the invisible world, shrines were established as sacred places to which the kami could be invited and where man could experience their presence.

This world in which we live is progressing from chaos to order, from the confusion of contradictions to a state of harmony and unity. Just as organic life develops, so in society good order is evolving as the result of mutual aid and cooperation. Shinto believes that this world gives promise of an unlimited development of life-power.

The world of Shinto is not an isolated one. It is an all-inclusive one. It includes all things organic and inorganic. All nature—man, animals, mountains, rivers, herbs and trees —come into existence by virtue of the kami, and their limitless blessings should contribute to the well-being of the world.

The world is not in contrast with nor in opposition to man. On the contrary, it is filled with the blessings of the kami and is developing through the power of harmony and cooperation. Shinto is not a pessimistic faith. It is an optimistic faith. This world is inherently good. That which interferes with man's happiness should be expelled. It belongs to another world.

Man Man is a child of kami, he also is inherently good. Yet there is no clear line of distinction between himself and the kami. In one sense men are kami, in another they will become kami. Man owes his life, which is sacred, to the kami and to his ancestors. He is loved and protected by them. He is endowed with the life and spirit of the kami, but at the same time he receives his life from his parents, grandparents, and ancestors through countless ages. Man is dependent for his continued existence on both nature and society. He is a social being. He cannot live in isolation.

Man owes gratitude to the kami and his ancestors for his life, and for their all-encompassing love. He also owes much to his present family, his community, and the nation. His life is full of blessings and so he must accept his obligations to society and contribute to the vital development of all things entrusted to him.

Man possesses a personality, which is distinct in each individual. To this personality given by the kami there is added the tradition of the family and the contributions of many individuals and the society in which he lives. These together constitute his characteristics.

There is no place for egotism in Shinto. Egotism runs counter to the spirit of worship. Worship makes the interest of the community and public welfare paramount. This does not mean that the rights of the individual and the family are ignored. On the contrary, against the background of religious rites, the nature of the individual and the authority of the family are fully supported by society. The spirit of the people guarantees this.

Man is born with a purpose, a mission, in life. On the one hand, he has the responsibility of realizing the hopes and ideals of his ancestors. On the other hand, he has the inescapable duty of treating his descendants with even greater love and care, so that they too may realize the hopes and ideals of the ancestral spirits. Ancestors and descendants are lineally one. Reverence for ancestors must never be neglected. It is the only way in which man's life can be lived which will fulfill the reason for his coming into this world.

In order that man may be his best, he is theoretically regarded as kami. He is blessed with words of praise, with the power of words (*kotodama*), which can bring about a transformation in his character. In practice, however, men are not as a rule called kami until after death, when they achieve a new dimension.

Ethics: Good and Evil The pattern for the behavior of the people, individually and communally, was at first transmitted orally from generation to generation. Later it was set down in such records as the *Kojiki, Nihon Shoki,* and the *Taiho-ryo* which were accepted as standards.

The stability of ancient Japanese society was maintained by the requirements of traditions and customs, which were flexible and could respond to the demands of each new age. Thus, moral judgements as to what was considered to be good or bad were not a fixed system of standards, but varied considerably depending on each specific situation. The Shinto manner of grasping truth takes into consideration the fact that values are constantly changing. For example, in Shinto ethics nothing—sex, wealth, killing, etc.,—is regarded as unconditionally evil.

Under the clan system, in which the members of each community were bound together by a common blood relationship, mutual understanding prevailed rather generally and social order was maintained by somewhat simple standards consonant with the relatively simple social organization then in existence. Within social units having a common blood or geographical relationship there were relatively few anti-social elements. The spiritual center of society was in the kami-rites. Human relations were essentially the relationship of those who mutually served the kami. Human behavior was to a large extent determined by the relationship established in performing the kami-rites, that is, worship (*matsuri*).

However, when continental civilization, including Buddhism

and Confucianism, was introduced, social life in Japan became more complicated and the development of a legal system and the organization of a state which stressed ethical government became necessary. Moreover, Shinto became mixed with Confucianism, so that all clear distinctions were lost. Thus, purely Shinto conceptions of behavior disappeared, but the ethical attitude produced by the kami-rites survived and is relatively unchanged even today.

In ancient Shinto the concept of moral good and evil, good and bad fortune, good and bad quality in material were all expressed in terms meaning to have or to lack worldly value: *yoshi* (good) and *ashi* (bad). The soul of man is good. Shinto does not have the concept of original sin. Man by nature is inherently good, and the world in which he lives is good. This is the kami-world. Evil then cannot originate in man or in this world. It is an intruder. Evil comes from without. The source of temptation and evil is the world of darkness. The cause is evil spirits, called *magatsuhi*. Evil caused by *magatsuhi* is called *maga*. Moral evil is thus an affliction,—a temporary affliction. While man's soul is good, the flesh and senses readily succumb to temptation. Man commits evil because he has lost, has been deprived of, the capacity for normal action.

In modern Shinto there is no fixed and unalterable moral code. Good and evil are relative. The meaning and value of an action depends on its circumstances, motives, purpose, time, place, etc. Generally speaking, however, man's heart must be sincere; his conduct must be courteous and proper;

an evil heart, selfish desire, strife, and hatred must be removed; conciliation must be practiced; and feelings of goodwill, cooperation and affection must be realized. That which disturbs the social order, causes misfortune, and obstructs worship of the kami and the peaceful development of this world of kami is evil. Sin and evil, including disasters, pollution, and even the abnormal are all caused by evil spirits which must be exorcised. Therefore, it is necessary to distinguish clearly between good and evil.

That by which good and evil can be distinguished is the soul of man. This distinction is made possible by the help of the kami. A correct judgement, one which accords with the mind of the kami, is possible when there is a state of unity between the divine and the human, when man can approach the kami with a clear bright mind in worship.

Salvation The world of the kami does not transcend that of man, and man does not need to seek to enter a divine, transcendental world to attain salvation. He seeks salvation by bringing the kami into the human world, into the daily life of the home, the market place, and the cooperation of the people. Man experiences the kami in this world and salvation is attained in the harmonious development of the world. This is epitomized in the myths in which the kami descend from the sacred heavenly country. (Takama-ga-hara) to the world of man, which is also the abode of the kami. In worship (*matsuri*), the spirits (*reikon*), the kami, and ancestral spirits are invited to the shrine or to some purified place from the High Heavenly Plain, the Eternal Country; and the evil spirits (*magatsuhi*) are expelled, because they interfere with man's relations with and approach to the kami and ancestral spirits. Therefore, before worship is possible there must be purification. The rite of purification drives away evil, the intruder. But purification does not relieve a person of responsibility for his past acts. On the contrary, it lays this upon him anew. By restoring the original nature of man, one will restore this capacity to do good. At the same time he will become sensible of the obligation to expiate evil and will become able to make amends for his past sins and failures.

Death In Shinto life is good, death is evil; but because for so many centuries funeral rites have been conducted almost exclusively by Buddhist priests, people today, even many Japanese, are unaware of the Shinto attitude towards death or the fact that funerals are conducted in accordance with Shinto rites.

Shinto regards death as evil or a curse; but it is incorrect to say that the reason shrines have no contact with the dead or rites for the dead is in order to avoid pollution. As a matter of fact, although Shinto regards death as an evil, it does not necessarily regard it as pollution. For example, the word *kegare*, which is used in reference to death also means " abnormality " or " misfortune." Moreover, when relatives or superiors died, officials were given a day off and people were excused from the service at shrine affairs. Shinto priests, however, devoted themselves to the service of the kami, and so did not become involved in funeral services. In ancient times funerals were conducted by the people themselves in accordance with Shinto rites. Moreover, in some few cases there are graves either within the shrine precinct itself or immediately adjacent and it appears that some shrines originally were built in front of burial mounds. Furthermore, there are a great many shrines devoted to commemoration of the departed spirits of historical persons. The Tenmangu shrines are dedicated to the spirit of the great scholar, Michizane Sugawara, the Toshogu shrines to Ieyasu Tokugawa; the Nogi Shrine to General Maresuke Nogi of Russo-Japanese War fame; the Ninomiya Shrine to Sontoku Ninomiya, the economist and moral teacher and Yasukuni Shrine and many local shrines to the veneration and consolation of those who made the supreme sacrifice for their country. Thus Shinto, that should treat all ancestral spirits in the same way and worship them as kami, under the impact of Buddhism which has pre-empted the place of Shinto in this field, today generally enshrines only a limited number of those who served the state and society.

The ancient Japanese believed that the dead continued to live as spirits (*reikon*) and from time to time visited this world, received services (rites) from their descendants, and in turn blessed them. As expressions of happiness and gratitude to the ancestral spirits, fine tombs were built for the dead and at harvest time festivals were conducted and offerings of first fruits were presented. This was an integral part of the Shinto faith and the duty of all people.

With the introduction of Chinese civilization and the consequent spread of Buddhism, however, the building of gigantic tombs and the conduct of elaborate funerals was restricted. But ancient customs and beliefs could not be swept away, so Buddhism adapted itself to Japanese ideas and incorporated the indigenous customs regarding the dead into its rituals. Thus, the care of tombs, the chanting of sutras like magic formulae, and the presentation of offerings, as well as belief in rebirth in the Pure Land, became an integral part of Japanese Buddhism.

This was a relatively simple development at first, because the bodies of the dead were not permitted within shrine precincts and shrine priests did not as a rule concern themselves with funeral rites. Then in later centuries Buddhism became further entrenched in this field because the Tokugawa government (1603—1868), in connection with its suppression of Christianity, required all people to be buried exclusively by Buddhist priests. Consequently Buddhism, which fundamentally is opposed to such practices, became preoccupied with funerals and memorial services, and the fact that these were originally indigenous customs based on Shinto ideas has been generally forgotten.

There were two reasons why shrine priests did not concern themselves with the dead and with funeral rites. In the first place, the Shrines were dedicated to the service of the enshrined kami, and were not places for other rites or functions. In the second place, the priests were devoted solely to the service of the enshrined kami. Therefore, generally speaking, the performance of religious rites for other than the enshrined kami was outside the responsibility of the shrines and the priesthood.

During the Meiji era and subsequently, government regulations prohibited the priests of shrines of the higher grades from performing funerals, but this restriction no longer exists and services are frequently conducted by priests irrespective of the shrine they serve. However, the services are conducted at homes or in public funeral halls. They are never held in shrines or even in shrine precincts.

Universal Nature of Shinto

Shinto is a racial religion. It is inextricably interwoven with the fabric of Japanese customs and ways of thinking. It is impossible to separate it from the communal and national life of the people. Among the kami of Shrine Shinto many have a special claim to worship from the Japanese people alone and are not such as can be venerated by the peoples of the world in the sense that the Japanese people do. Although non-Japanese may pay great respect to the Emperor Meiji, for example, it is inconceivable that they should ever regard him as a kami in the same sense as do the Japanese. Therefore, this phase of the kami-faith is not suitable for dissemination abroad.

But this does not mean that there is no concern in Shinto for the people and welfare of mankind; nor does it mean that Shinto is not worthy of respect from those of other faiths in the world at large. People of all races and climes cannot help but express gratitude to the spirits of the land and of nature, to their ancestors, to the benefactors of society and the state. In so far as they recognize this feeling within them, they cannot but understand the spirit of Shinto, and find in it an undeniable truth which supports and heightens man's noblest values. Thus, while Shinto is a racial faith, it possesses a universality which can enrich the lives of all people everywhere.

INDEX

ablution pavilion 34

Ama-terasu-ō-mikami 天照大神 4

Ame-no-minakanushi-no-kami 天御中主神 4

approach 31, 32

architecture 35—40; styles of(-*zukuri* 造), Gion 祇園, Hachiman 八幡, Gongen 権現, Hiyoshi日吉, Irimoya 入母屋, Kasuga 春日, Nagare 流 38, Ōtori 大鳥, Shinmei 神明, Sumiyoshi 住吉, Taisha 大社, Tenchi Kongen 天地根元, Yatsumune 八棟

asa-gutsu 浅沓 45

ashi 悪し 106

Association of Shinto Shrines 17, 18, 42, 43, 65, 81, 89

banners 25

bell 22, 61

Buddhism 72, 73, 78, 79, 85, 89, 106, 108, 109, 110

bugaku 舞楽 67, 68, 71, 83

caves 101

ceremonies 50 ff,

charms 35

Charter Oath: Gokajō no Goseimon 五箇条の御誓文 73

chigi 千木 36—37, 38

Christianity 89, 110

Confucianism 85, 78, 106

Crown Prince, wedding of 13, 76

death 102, 108

deer 33

eboshi 烏帽子 45

Emperor 79—82; Jimmu 神武 5, 38 80, 101; Kammu 桓武 80; Kazan 花山 41; Kōmei 弘明 80; Meiji 明治 73, 80, 81, 111; Ōjin 応神 80

Engi Shiki 延喜式 11, 56

Enryakuji 延暦寺 86

entertainment 71

evil 72

feast, symbolic 51, 57

festival 祭 50 ff. annual-: *reisai* 例祭 63, Boys- 90, Gion- 祇園 70, Girls- 90, Jidai- 時代 70, Star- 90

fox 33

fuda 札 62

funerals 57, 108

gagaku 雅楽 83

gates 30, 32

gohei 御幣 24, 68

gon-gūji 権宮司 42, *gon-negi* 権禰宜 42

good and evil 105—6

graves 27

gūji 宮司 42

Hakkō Ichi-u 八紘一宇 81

halberd 25

harai 祓 51—2

haraigushi 祓串 24

Hirata, Atsutane 平田篤胤 87

Hokkaido Jinja Kyōkai, 北海道神社協会 18

horses, sacred: *shinme* 神馬 33, 55

hyakudo ishi 百度石 34

ichiba 市場 85

images of kami: *shinzō* 神像 24

Imbe 忌部 14, 41

Imperial Family 8, 13, 15, 75, 76, 79, 80, 81

Imperial messenger: *chokushi* 勅使 14, 41, 65, 70

Imperial Palace shrines: Kyūchū-sanden 宮中三殿 13

Imperial Regalia: *Sanshu no Shinki* 三種の神器 13

Inari shrines 稲荷神社 29, 33

Inari, Toyokawa 豊川稲荷 88
Ise, Grand Shrine of 6, 13, 15, 23,
    34, 35, 36, 42, 47, 58, 81, 83, 94,
    96, 98; Inner Shrine: Naikū 内宮
    37 High Priestess: *saishu* 祭主 42,
    Outer Shrine: Gekū 外宮 37;
    talisman: *taima* 58
Izanagi-no-mikoto 伊弉諾尊, 伊邪那岐
    命 4
Izanami-no-mikoto 伊弉冊尊, 伊邪那
    美命 4
Izumo, kami of 出雲神 5, 75, 95;
    Grand Shrine of- 出雲大社 21, 26,
    36
jewels: tama 玉 5, 64
Jingi Kai 神祇会 17
Jingi Kan 神祇官 41, 72
Jingū Hōsai Kai 神宮奉斎会 17
Jinja-chō 神社庁 18
Jinja Honchō 神社本庁 17, 18
Jinja Honkyō 神社本教 18
Jinnō Shōtōki 神皇正統記 23
jōtō-sai 上棟祭 90
kannabi 神奈備 98
kankokuhei-sha 官国幣社 73
kagura 神楽 45, 62, 66, 67, 71, 83;
kami 6, 9, 50; guardian 9, 32, 47
kami-dana 神棚 58
Kami-musubi-no-mikoto 神皇産霊尊,
    -kami 神産巣日神 4
kanmuri 冠 45
kan-nigiwai 神賑 71
kariginu 狩衣 44
Kashiko-dokoro 賢所 13
katsuogi 鰹木 36, 37
kegare 穢 108
kessai 潔斎 64
Kiso Mitake Honkyō 木曾御嶽本教 18
Kitabatake, Chikafusa 北畠親房 23
kindergartens 96, 97
Kirisutokyō Rengō Kai 基督教連合会
    83

kotodama 言霊 104
Kogoshūi 古語拾遺 11
Kojiki 古事記 4, 10, 11, 78, 101
Kokugakuin Daigaku 国学院大学 40
koma inu 狛犬 22
Kongōbuji 金剛峯寺 86
Kono-hana-sakayahime-no-mikoto 木
    花咲耶姫命 100
Kōrei-den 皇霊殿 13
kōsha 講社 95
Kōten Kōkyū Sho 皇典講究所 17
Kujiki 旧事紀 11
Kyōbu Shō 教部省 73
lanterns 34
maga 禍 107
magatama 曲玉 64
magatsuhi 禍津日 102, 106
man 102—103
matsuri 祭 50 ff., 106, 107; *matsuri-
    goto* 祭事 76
Meiji Restoration 明治維新 72, 87
miko 巫女 43, 66
mikoshi 神輿 26, 68
Ministry of Education 43, 74
mirror 5, 13, 22, 23
misogi 禊 52
mitamashiro 霊代 21
monkey 33
mochi 餅 66
Moon Goddess 4, 5
mori 森 98
Motoori, Norinaga 本居宣長 87
mountain, sacred 99
Mount Fuji 富士山 95, 100; Ontake
    御嶽 95; Nantai 男体 101
music 67
musicians 41, 44
mythology 4, 6
Nakatomi 中臣 14, 41
naorai 直会 51, 57, 66
nationalism 78
nature 97

negi 禰宜 42

Nihongi 日本紀, *Nihon Shoki* 日本書紀 2, 3, 10, 11, 77, 105

Nihon Kyōha Shintō Renmei 日本教派神道連盟 88

Nihon Shūkyō Kyōryoku Kyōgi Kai 日本宗教協力協議会 88

neighborhood associations 49

Nikkō 日光 31, 70, 98, 101

Ninigi-no-mikoto 瓊瓊杵尊 5, 13, 23, 75, 100

Niō-san (or *-sama*) 仁王さん 32

Noh 能 83

norito 祝詞 5, 55, 56, 77

nursery schools 96

Occupation, Allied 15, 16, 17, 74

offering hall: *shinsen-den* 神饌殿 26

offerings *shinsen* 神饌 51—53, 59

Ōharai 大祓 52

Ōkuni-nushi-no-kami 大国主神 5, 75

oracles, printed: *mikuji* 御籤 62

oratory: *haiden* 拝殿 26

oshi 御師 94, 95

otabisho 御旅所 69

parish 46—48; parishioners 46—48

prayers 26, 51, 55

precincts: *keidai* 境内 27—28, 32

priest: *shinshoku* 神職, *kan-nushi* 神主 40, 42—44; costumes 44—46; prayer-priests 94, quarters: *saikan* 祭官 26, shaman 40, women priests 40

processions: *goshinkō* 御神幸 67—70

playgrounds 97

purification 24, 34, 51, 52, 108

reikon 霊魂 107, 109

reisai 例祭 63

rocks 101

saikai 斎戒 64

saisei itchi 祭政一致 73, 76

sakaki 榊 24, 52, 58, 62, 64, 66, 99

salvation 102, 107

sanctuary: *shinden* 神殿, *honden* 本殿 21

sandō 参道 31—32;

Sannō Ichijitsu 山王一実, -Shintō 神道 87

Sarume 猿女 41

scriptures 9, 12

Sectarian (Kyōha 教派) Shinto 12

shaku 笏 45

shaman 40

shimenawa 七五三縄 25, 35

Shin-den 神殿 13

shinkai 神界 69

shinkyō 神鏡 68

Shin Nippon Shūkyō Dantai Rengō Kai 新日本宗教団体連合会 88

shintai 神体 21, *-zan* 神体山 99

Shirakawa 白河 41

Shinto 2—3; Directive 15, 16, 17, 74; type of: Domestic 12; Imperial Household 13; Ise 87; Popular 12; Revival 87; Sannō 山王 87; Sectarian 12, 73, 95; Shrine 14, 15, 48, 79; State 15; Watarai 渡会 87; Yoshida 吉田 87; Yuitsu 唯一 87; Universal Nature of 111

Shrine Association of Kyoto 18

shrine organizations 17—18; -office: *shamusho* 社務所 26

Shrines: Akama 赤間 31; Dazaifu 太宰府 47; Enoshima 江島 101; Fuji Sengen 富士浅間 38; Fushimi Inari 伏見稲荷 29, 55, 96; Futara 二荒 101; Hachiman 八幡 29, 87; Heian 平安 47, 70; Hiyoshi 日吉 33, 86; Ise (see Ise); Itsukushima 厳島 102; Izumo Taisha 出雲大社 75; Kashiwara 橿原 38; Kibitsu 吉備津 38; Kirishima 霧島 27; Kitano 北野 40; Kumano 熊野 102; Meiji 明治 38, 47, 70; Mitsumine 三峯 33; Miyazaki 宮崎 80; Nibutsu Hime 丹生都比売 86 ; Ninomiya 二宮 109 ; Nogi 乃木 108 ; Ōmiwa 大神 20, 21, 30, 100 ; Ōyama 大山 31 Suwa 諏訪 102 ; Ten'itsu 天一 99 ; Tōshōgū 東照宮 87, 98, 109 ; Udo 鵜戸 101 ; Yasaka 八坂 70 ; Yasu-kuni 靖国 23, 43, 47

Shugendō 修験道 101

statistics 43

sukeisha 崇敬者 47

suiten-mon 水天門 31

Sun Goddess 4, 13, 15, 23

Susano-o-no-mikoto 素戔嗚尊, 須佐之男命 4

Sword, sacred 5, 25

Taihō-ryō 大宝令 105

Takama-ga-hara 高天原 102, 107

Taka-mimusubi-no-mikoto 高皇産霊尊, -kami 高御産巣日神 4

talisman : *fuda* 62

tamagushi 玉串 55

temizu 手水 52, -ya 手水舎 34

Tokoyo-no-kuni 常世国 102

Tokugawa, Ieyasu 徳川家康 70

torii 鳥居 1, 28, 29, 30, 31, 60 ; types of- 30

tree worship 35, 98, 99 ; sacred tree : *shinboku* 神木 35, 99

Tsuki-yomi-no-mikoto 月読尊 4

ujigami 氏神 9, 47 ; *ujiko* 氏子 47

Urabe 卜部 41

waterfalls (Nachi 那智) 102

wolf 33

women attendants : *ujiko* 43, 45, 66, priests 43

worship 50 ff., 104, worship hall : *haiden* 拝殿 100

Yabusame 流鏑馬 71

Yamabushi 山伏 101

Yata-no-kagami 八咫鏡 13

Yomi-no-kuni 黄泉国 102

yoshi 善し 106

Yoshida, Kanetomo 吉田兼倶 87

Zen Nippon Bukkyō Kai 全日本仏教会 88